HAUNTED
SALISBURY

HAUNTED SALISBURY

Frogg Moody & Richard Nash

For Diana Nora Nash (1937–2011)
who left us with so much –
including an open mind

In memory of my late father,
Jack Moody, whose spirit lives on

First published 2012

The History Press
The Mill, Brimscombe Port
Stroud, Gloucestershire, GL5 2QG
www.thehistorypress.co.uk

© Frogg Moody & Richard Nash, 2012

The right of Frogg Moody & Richard Nash to be identified as the
Authors of this work has been asserted in accordance with the
Copyrights, Designs and Patents Act 1988.

British Library Cataloguing in Publication Data.
A catalogue record for this book is available from the British Library.

ISBN 978 0 7524 8645 1
Typesetting and origination by The History Press
Printed in Great Britain

Contents

Foreword

GHOSTS, ghouls, spirits, spectres, spooks, things that go bump in the night – all have provided an endless source of oral and psychic fascination for generations. Ever since our ancient ancestors confined their dead to the afterlife, the spirit world has proved to be a potent influence to people across many parts of the world; and still is, despite increased secular attitudes in modern society. Some souls have proved to be more restless than others and have refused to lie down. All have returned to some of our most familiar and often unlikely locations to visit present generations.

Tales of the supernatural abound right here in our own city of Salisbury: locations within sight of the spire and the surrounding area, phantoms in public houses, victims of macabre murder, condemned traitors and convicted felons. Also many tales that have never been told before, which are now contained within the pages of this book, shrouded behind a fascinating historical background.

Believer or sceptic, ghost stories exist in abundance. Few people have failed to meet someone who has not encountered a ghost, an apparition or inexplicable presence within a room. For many, such encounters can produce life-changing results. These stories may inspire the reader to view local landmarks with new eyes, to enjoy, read or merely dip into; whatever the interest, ghost stories remain some of the most captivating stories ever told.

Phil Harding
Channel 4 Time Team
Wessex Archaeology

The imposing thirteenth-century Salisbury Cathedral at dusk.
(Alan Clarke)

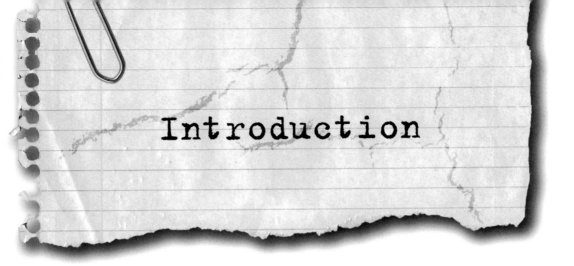

Introduction

IN south Wiltshire, the shadows of human existence fall long and wide. The river valleys leading to Salisbury Plain in the north and the royal hunting grounds of Cranborne Chase and the New Forest in the south are littered with forts and earthworks, tumuli and churches, memorials and plaques. From the mysteries of Stonehenge, which lifetimes have been spent unravelling, to the achievements of twentieth-century pop stars, the region has played its part in every significant period of British history.

Within this context Salisbury, which dominates the area in terms of population, employment, recreation and culture, is a relatively modern city. The classic medieval grid-patterned streets were initially built up around the thirteenth-century Cathedral Church of the Blessed Virgin Mary, which had replaced an older cathedral sited at nearby Old Sarum, after Bishop Poore fell out with Henry III.

This oldest part of the new city does however have an atmosphere of great antiquity and with this comes the stories – the mysteries, witches and curses and … the ghosts. Even the cathedral itself has its legends.

It is said that when Bishop Poore was seeking a site for his new cathedral, he asked an archer to fire an arrow from Old Sarum in to the valley below, and where it landed so fate would decree the building should begin. How did the arrow fly for two miles? The legend has it that, by chance, the arrow struck a deer, which ran on for some distance before expiring. Then there was the theory, expounded across 1940s playgrounds, that Salisbury had not been Blitzed as Adolf Hitler intended to marry Eva Braun in the cathedral.

The cynic might argue that the bishop selected his building site for the lushness and sheltered nature of the fields in this part of the Avon Valley (which he happened to own), and the Luftwaffe found the cathedral spire a useful landmark on its way to Bristol and the Midlands – but this isn't a book for cynics.

At the heart of the city lies the Market Place and the street names in the surrounding area reflect this – Cheese Market, Fish Row, Ox Row. At the western end of Butcher Row sits the fifteenth-century Poultry Cross, the last survivor of the city's four market crosses, and it is here that we find our first spirit.

To the amateur ghost hunter he can be difficult to spot, as he does not walk through walls or float around in historic clothing, and has not lost any body parts. Rather, he stands under the cross in a modern, three-piece grey suit, unassuming and quiet but with a somehow slightly disturbing air of otherworldliness. He then disappears in an instant, but to where? And why from here? Perhaps he is simply waiting for the Haunch of Venison to open.

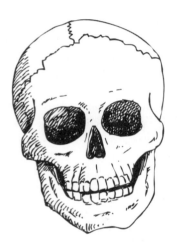

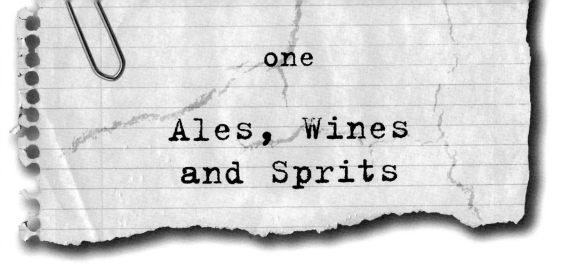

one

Ales, Wines
and Sprits

The Haunted Pubs of Salisbury

The famous Haunch of Venison sits in Minster Street, almost opposite the Poultry Cross. The inn was first built in 1320, apparently to provide lodgings for those employed in adding the spire to the cathedral.

The Haunch of Venison, Salisbury's most haunted pub and home to the famous mummified hand. (Elliott Tunnard)

Whether you are looking at it from street level or ensconced in one of its odd little rooms, the Haunch feels as if it were haphazardly built on an indeterminate number of levels, with odd passages leading here and there, and it seems to creak – and even sometimes sway – like an old ship. Indeed, some of the building's oak beams are thought to have been salvaged from sailing vessels.

The odd arrangement of the rooms is attributed to the original use of the building, as the more senior masons and foremen occupied the upper floors, with the lower class of labourer living below. An upper floor retains the name 'The House Of Lords' as a result of this tradition.

Tiles in the bar of the inn are said to have once been part of the fabric of the cathedral, and the pewter bar top is thought to be the last surviving complete example of its kind in England. The fireplace of the main dining room bears the date of the Spanish Armada – 1588.

A number of interesting sixteenth- and seventeenth-century artefacts have been discovered when work has been carried out on the building at various times:

a Queen Elizabeth silver groat, two playing cards (the queen and ten of clubs), a stoneware wine flagon (bearing a cipher of three hearts), a rodent trap, a shoe showing signs of having been gnawed by a rat, a lady's shoe and a half-pint pewter pot engraved with the name of a landlady, Louisa Potts. A number of these items were donated to what has become the Salisbury & South Wiltshire Museum.

In the spring of 1944 the Haunch's smallest bar, to the immediate right of the Minster Street entrance, was used by Winston Churchill and General Dwight Eisenhower during their preparations for the impending invasion of Europe. A rather public place for such a sensitive plan one might have thought –

but on the other hand two such large characters armed with sheaves of maps of the Normandy coastline would have left little space in this tiny room for any flapping ears or tongues.

In any case, given the long established extent of military installations around the city, the citizens of Salisbury were perhaps simply used to the sight of top brass and manoeuvres in the area. Roy Nash, an inquisitive Highbury Avenue schoolboy at the time of the D-Day preparations, recalls that all the local playing fields and woods were completely filled with personnel, equipment, machinery and ammunition – but the general populace had no idea of what was about to happen.

Inside the Haunch of Venison, which dates back to 1320. (Timezone Collection)

The mummified hand was found by workmen in 1903 still holding playing cards. (Timezone Collection)

The ghosts that haunt the Haunch are not linked to these historical events. The most celebrated has been dubbed 'The Demented Whist Player' although the real name of the individual involved in the story is not recorded. One evening in the 1820s this man arrived in Salisbury, whilst travelling from Southampton to an unknown destination, and sought lodgings at the Haunch of Venison.

The Haunch was renowned as 'An Old English Chop House', a title that, in earlier times, had only been given to very high-class eating establishments. What happened there on this particular evening would put a whole new slant on the meaning of 'chop'. These events were recorded in a ballad entitled 'The Hand at the Haunch'.

The regular patrons were drinking, talking heartily, playing cards and shove

11

ha'penny but, as the stranger entered the room, the throng fell dead silent, in the best traditions of a true 'local'. Unmoved, the stranger strode to the bar and ordered a tankard of ale, which he drank straight down. He then tossed a gold coin to the pot boy and ordered more ale for all. This eased the tension and the stranger was invited to join a card game.

After a few rounds of 'win some and lose some', the stranger's luck began to improve and he started to win hand on hand. Silence returned to the room. Soon the stranger had won the price of his lodgings for the night … and five times the cost of the round of drinks he had bought.

A butcher, with a seat at the game quite close to the stranger, was growing both suspicious and angry. He drew a blade and with a single expert chop struck off the man's right hand. With the stranger screaming in pain and shock, the other players looked to the rush-strewn floor where the hand had fallen … and saw that it held five aces.

In 1903 a mummified hand, holding playing cards, was found by builders working at the Haunch and was preserved in a glass cabinet. Although this is traditionally believed to have been the extremity removed from the stranger, it was not holding a winning hand from any recognisable card game, and theories have also been put forward that it could have been a 'Hand of Glory'.

A Hand of Glory was a candle made from, or sitting in, a dead man's hand, and would be used in the practice of witchcraft or sorcery. A 'recipe' for the device was published in France in 1772: the hand would be obtained from a hanged felon whilst the body was still on the gibbet. It was then wrapped in part of a funeral pall before being squeezed to obtain the pulp, which was then refashioned into the shape of a hand, containing a wick that, once lit, had great secret power.

The Haunch made international headlines when the hand was stolen in 2010. Following the publicity, the artefact was returned in a bubble envelope, courtesy of the Royal Mail. Manager Justina Miller recalls that, 'The girl who opened it had a shock. We were expecting a pump for the beer – she opened it and just screamed "Oh my God! The hand!"'

The stranger's restless spirit – sinister by virtue of both its very presence and, presumably, its enforced left-handedness – has walked the myriad floors of the Haunch for nigh on two centuries. Perhaps to attempt to prove his innocence, perhaps to warn other visitors to curb any urge to cheat the men of Salisbury, or perhaps to simply take his revenge and retrieve his winnings and 'personalised' deck of cards … and his hand of course.

Whatever his motives, the spirit hides objects, moves glasses across tables, opens and closes doors and switches taps, lights and electric appliances on and off. These actions are usually accompanied by a strong smell of freshly turned earth.

Dave Taylor lodged at the Haunch in around 1980, in two rooms at the top of the building – rumoured locally to have been where Sir Walter Raleigh wrote his gallows speech whilst in transit to the Tower of London. Dave recalls how even on a very warm night the top bar of the inn would suddenly turn cold:

… as if something extremely chilly had just shot across the room from one corner and out of the door. Nothing was visible but most people in the room would stop and look at each other as if to say 'What was that?'

Also, on the second set of stairs – leading off the kitchen area – there was always a fairly rank smell of fat until you got to the middle of the stairs, where in

The haunted stairs where many people have witnessed the strange aroma of freshly turned earth and grass. (Timezone Collection)

a very small, localised area there was a smell of freshly turned earth and grass – a definite smell of 'the outside'. I say 'localised' because this smell occupied a definite space – shoe box sort of sized – that if you put your head in you could smell it and if you moved your head back a few inches you could smell the kitchen again.

The current manager of the Haunch, Justina Miller, now lives in the same flat at the top of the building:

One night I woke up and saw a middle-aged guy stood by my bed with his arms crossed like this [across his chest], just watching, in old brown trousers and a shirt.

I have a shelf on the wall with a box on it, and I had an angel in there. A couple of months later I heard a very big bang. I woke up and my boyfriend said 'Don't worry, it was just the wind', but the next day he said, 'I didn't want to scare you but there was a guy stood by the bed' – and we exactly, step-by-step, described the same guy. It was impossible that the box would have fallen off the shelf from the wind, but the box was on the floor and the angel had the head snapped off. Another lady living here saw the same guy – legend has it that it is the card player – he always has his arms crossed so you can't see his hands.

Justina has had many odd experiences during her five years at the Haunch:

Just little things like knocking sounds, and the door handles turning and feeling like something is walking with you or is around you – you know you are not alone. Sometimes you don't hear anything for months, and then it kicks off again.

One night I locked up the restaurant – it was all set up with the white napkins. Next morning I unlocked the door – I had been alone in the building, but suddenly the napkins were red. Another time three whisky glasses had appeared on the floor of the restaurant.

A second, more innocent and pitiful, ghost is also often seen at the Haunch. Around the cusp of the Victorian and Edwardian eras, a young boy was sent by his mother to buy bottles of drink at the inn. It is not known whether the lad ran away, was kidnapped or murdered, or simply met with an accident – but he never came home again.

When the boy's mother later came to the inn to ask about her son, she was told he had never arrived. Each day she would walk around the area looking for the child until, eventually, she became ill and met her own death. Since that time her spirit, clad in a white shawl, has continued the search both in the pub and along Minster Street.

Justina Miller remembers an incident from her earliest days at the Haunch:

I woke up and saw a lady in my room. She was just walking past. She had a long white dress and black hair – she just glided across the room like a swan. I told Dave, the cleaner, in the morning that I thought I was going crazy, but he said, 'Oh she probably just came to say hello' and told me all the stories. The last time I saw her was on Christmas Day [2011] – just walking down the stairs. She had her hair up and I followed her thinking one of the customers had got lost – and then I realised there were no ladies in the bar.

Dave is like a friend to the ghost. He has seen her so many times just in passing: in the gents toilets, in this room, in the kitchen and quite often in the restaurant. He also says

The alleyway to the rear of the Haunch of Venison. The Grey Lady has been seen in this location. (Timezone Collection)

he can smell her when she comes in, and another customer who has drunk here for twenty years is always saying about the smell – like the smell of flowers or something.

One sceptical customer saw the lady at about 1 a.m. one Christmas morning. The woman had asked Justina about the stories surrounding the inn, but scoffed at what she was told. However, after a visit to the ladies' toilets she returned shaking and sobbing, having seen the spirit of the lady in white sat in the corner of the House of Lords.

James Beret, an early eighteenth-century landlord of the Haunch of Venison, is said to have turned raving mad. This eventuality could quite possibly have arisen from his having drunk too much of his own cheap gin. However, his descent into madness might have been accelerated by regular sightings of the grey lady who walks among the graves of the nearby churchyard.

A door at the rear of the inn leads onto an alley, beyond which is the church of St Thomas à Becket. The original church on this site was one of the very first buildings to be built in the city of New Sarum. Originally constructed of wood, the church was especially built to allow workmen, camping in nearby meadows while they worked on the new cathedral, to have a place of worship.

The Haunch of Venison is thought to have once formed part of the incumbent's church house. There is also a rumour that (for the benefit of the reputation of the clergy) an underground tunnel once ran between the church and the inn, which at that particular time was, reputedly, hosting a brothel.

Were the grey lady's services among the specialties of the house and does she, having been banished from the church by a red-faced customer, walk the grounds awaiting her revenge? Or does her eternal torment simply arise from her having been one of the innumerable everyday mortal sinners who have sat in the church and recognised the inevitable result of their own actions, so graphically set out in the famous Doom Painting?

Dating from around 1475, the painting is arranged around the chancel arch and shows Christ on the day of judgement, sending the souls of the righteous to Heaven and those of the wicked to Hell. The Damned are portrayed on the right side of the arch, watched over by the Devil. The tip of the Prince of Darkness' clawed foot is the only element that projects out of the main area of the picture. It creeps across the otherwise bare stone of the tracery … beckoning … reminding all who watch that, even in the house of God, the Devil need not obey the rules.

The Devil has his arms around a 'dishonest ale-wife', who is holding a jug – perhaps obtained at the Haunch of Venison. Below, a group of chained souls, including one wearing a bishop's mitre and two wearing crowns, is dragged into the mouth of Hell, held agape by two horned devils. Also depicted is a miser with his money bags, dragged along by another devil, whose touch has left black burn-marks on the miser's shoulder.

Below is a depiction of a figure believed to be St Osmund, the Patron Saint of Salisbury, and a Latin scroll *Nulla est Redemptio* – 'There is no Redemption'. The wording of the scroll leaves no room for doubt when read in its normal context – *In Inferno Nulla est Redemptio* – 'In Hell There is no Redemption'.

Considering the age of many of the inns in Salisbury (and indeed the number that there once were) it is perhaps surprising that few of them seem to have had ghost stories handed down.

The Rai d'Or – once also known as the Star, in Brown Street, is said to house five friendly ghosts. The name of the premises has recently reverted to the name it went by in the Middle Ages. The present building was built in the sixteenth century, as a reconstruction of the original thirteenth-century tavern built, as so many buildings in and around the city centre were, for the benefit of workmen engaged in the building of Salisbury Cathedral.

The tavern's most famous tenant was probably Agnes Bottenham, who also ran a brothel from the premises, at a time when the nearby Love Lane was at the centre of the city's whoring trade. In 1370 Agnes gave land in Trinity Street, behind the tavern, for the foundation of Trinity Hospital as penance for her sins and to house retired prostitutes.

In 1998 a tunnel was discovered under the bar of the Rai d'Or, leading from the back of the building towards the cathedral – perhaps, as with the Haunch, this allowed the clergy to enter the premises without being seen. The corner tenement of the modern building retains traces of an external double staircase with a balcony, where the prostitutes would have displayed their charms. The building also retains a fine inglenook fireplace, where 'The Doctor' – one of the resident ghosts – can sometimes be seen.

The streets and alleyways around the old part of the city were the scene of skirmishes during the English Civil War, and no book of supernatural phenomena would be complete without at least one Cavalier story. A Royalist phantom is said to haunt the old Catherine Wheel public house, to the east of the Market Place in Milford Street – now known as The City Lodge.

Salisbury, as a city, was inclined to Parliament, whilst the cathedral was inclined to the King, and at various times Roundhead soldiers or Cavalier soldiers

Part of the famous 'Doom Painting' depicting Christ on judgement day. The painting dates from **c.**1475. *(Timezone Collection!)*

The Rai d'Or, once also known as the Star, in Brown Street. This colourful establishment is said to be the home to five ghosts and was once a brothel! (Timezone Collection)

would be seen around the town, depending on which side was having the upper hand.

Salisbury historian George Fleming believes that:

> Cavaliers would not have been popular with the good people of Salisbury, and Cavalier officers in particular were much worse behaved than Parliamentarian officers. Parliament, very early in the game decided that it needed discipline in its army – bible reading, no gambling, no swearing, no whoring – whereas the Cavalier lot were the opposite.

It is said that a bunch of Cavalier officers were once sitting in the Catherine Wheel, getting drunk and talking in a lewd and ungodly way. One of them was particularly outrageous and one of his friends warned that the Devil would surely take him one of these days, to which he replied along the lines of 'Damn me, if the Devil appeared now I would pull his ears' or something similar that showed great disrespect, whereupon, it is said, there was a clap of thunder and suddenly a large figure appeared, grabbed the offending Cavalier and flew out the window, never to be seen again.

It occurred to me that one possible explanation might be that it was a gunpowder accident – distressingly common in those days. They may have been mucking about with cartridges – for instance drying out damp cartridges by the fire – that was a common mistake. Another thing, if you were trying to show off, was throwing cartridges in to the fire. So it's possible that some Jack-the-Lad Cavalier blew himself up playing the fool with gunpowder and in later retellings the smoke, the bang and the dead Cavalier all became 'The Devil'.

It seems probable that this story is that recorded by John Bunyan in *The Life and Death of Mr Badman* in 1680. Although the inn is not named, Bunyan describes an incident in Salisbury in which a man 'in the midst of his health, drinking and carousing in a tavern' made a toast to the Devil and stated that, 'if the Devil would not come and pledge him, he would not believe that there was either God or Devil'. A little later the innkeeper, on 'hearing a hideous noise, and smelling a stinking savour', ran to the room, which he found to be empty, but with the window broken and the bar across it bent and covered in blood. His guest was never heard of again.

This Cavalier ghost seems to be that of a somewhat vulgar fellow, whereas his comrades from across the country are often portrayed as loyal, honest, unlucky and betrayed patriots — and often from high stock. Salisbury does have its 'noble' spirits — of birth if not necessarily of character — but, as we shall see in our next chapter, they originated in earlier times.

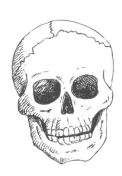

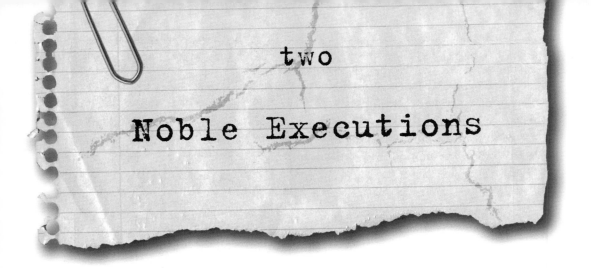

two

Noble Executions

The Traitorous Duke and the Murderous Lord

The Blue Boar Inn stood to the north of Salisbury's Market Place in what was once known as 'The Parade'. We are unfortunately no longer able to interrogate the inn's buildings to discover their history in the same way we can with the Haunch of Venison.

However, the Blue Boar enjoyed a high profile in the city for more than 300 years, until its demolition in 1756. Its near neighbour, the Saracen's Head, was demolished later, when the market area was widened – at the same time, The Parade was renamed Blue Boar Row. Despite its name living on in this way, the Blue Boar would perhaps be merely an entry on the list of lost inns, if it wasn't for the events of 1483.

The Blue Boar was a Yorkist emblem and was adopted by Richard, Duke of Gloucester and younger brother of Edward IV. Salisbury's Blue Boar ghost arises from actions taken by the duke once he had become Richard III. The accession of Richard took place after the two sons of Edward IV had been declared illegitimate. These sons – the fated 'Princes in the Tower'

The Duke of Buckingham plaque at Debenham's Store, Salisbury. (Timezone Collection)

– were eventually killed, although it is not known for certain whether this was by Richard's will or that of his eventual successor, Henry VII.

What is certain is that Richard was responsible for the death of Henry Stafford, the Duke of Buckingham. The extremely wealthy Buckingham was a cousin of Edward and Richard, and had assisted the latter in his taking of the throne.

However, Buckingham soon came to the view that the blood in his own veins gave him as much right to rule as Richard. He planned a coup and asked his supporters to muster at Bristol. The rebellion faltered when, whilst riding from North Wales, the duke's army was halted by the flooded river Severn, following a terrific storm that had engulfed the west of England.

His supporters having dispersed, Buckingham went into hiding. Following a betrayal by one of his followers, he was apprehended by the King's men and brought to Salisbury. He was lodged at the Blue Boar Inn – this establishment having the only rooms in the city that were both luxurious enough for nobility but secure enough for his confinement.

Richard was merciless and, having refused Buckingham an interview, ordered him to be beheaded the very next day, even though it would be a Sunday. The duke was however allowed the dignity of a private and swift execution – he was beheaded in the courtyard between the Blue Boar Inn and the Saracen's Head on 2 November.

The significance of the execution was recognised by William Shakespeare in Act V, Scene I of *The Life and Death of Richard III*, set in 'Salisbury. An Open Place'. This scene has Buckingham, on being led to the block by the sheriff, bemoaning the fact that 'All-Souls' day is my body's doomsday'.

A new building was constructed on the site in 1831, at which time human remains were found – a connection was immediately made with the Buckingham legend. Unfortunately, the remains were destroyed without the opportunity for investigation … but the head had been removed from the body. However, it has also been said that the remains of the duke were interred in the now destroyed church of the Grey Friars in London's Newgate Street. St Peter's church

The chest tomb at St Peter's church in Britford. It was once believed that Buckingham's remains were laid to rest here. (Alan Clarke)

in Britford, to the south of Salisbury, contains a chest tomb that at one time was believed to be that of Buckingham, but this theory has now been discredited.

Buckingham's head was apparently taken, still bleeding, to Richard, who was staying at a house in The Close – where bloodstains reappeared over the centuries. The building at the site of the duke's execution is now occupied by Debenhams, and to the rear of the old Blue Boar courtyard there remains an open space. Buckingham's ghost has been seen standing in this space and is said to have a somewhat melancholic air, although this must be a result of interpreting body language, given that the spirit is headless.

There have also been a number of strange occurrences within the building. During the Second World War, fire-watchers refused to stay here overnight and more recently, in June 2002, all the security alarms were set off and all the locked doors were flung wide open. On another occasion a telephone engineer was working in the attic room, where Buckingham was said to have been held, when he felt a cold touch on his shoulder. The terrified man ran out of the room and could not be persuaded to go back – somebody else had to retrieve his tools.

Whilst the duke's eternal misery permeates the building, the street to the front is said to be haunted by a happier spirit, a small girl dressed in Victorian clothes skipping around in a state of bliss. Other shops in Blue Boar Row are also haunted: 'Matilda' haunts the site at the corner with Endless Street – she is a teenage girl who is thought to have died of diphtheria and to be very interested in fashion. A lady in Edwardian dress haunts a shop between here and Debenhams. On one occasion she appeared through a locked door, approached the then proprietor and walked straight through him. A Cavalier with a red, plumed hat, named Oliver, walks the House of John A'Port in nearby Queen Street. When the building was occupied by Watson's fine china and giftware shop, he apparently became very fussy about how items were displayed, and moved them around if they didn't suit.

Buckingham was perhaps a victim of his own poor judgement: he had backed what seemed to be the right horse, but then decided he would rather ride it himself. By contrast our second noble spectre, the 8th Baron Stourton, was simply plain greedy.

Although the Stourton line was not one of particularly high nobility, the family was wealthy and well connected. In 1551 the 7th Baron, William, died. Before their marriage, his widow had been Lady Elizabeth Dudley, daughter of Edmund Dudley, the Duke of Northumberland.

Lady Elizabeth's dowry had been the source of the larger part of the Stourton fortunes which, on William's death, had reverted to her. Her riches would not pass to their son Charles, the 8th Baron, until such time as Elizabeth herself had passed. However, Charles, who by reputation had a foul temper and a propensity to violence, was impatient. He needed the means to maintain his debauched lifestyle, as well as to pay the debts he had already accrued in its pursuit.

With his father's body hardly cold, Charles visited his mother at Kilmington, to the west of Salisbury. He had devised a plan to convince her that a more rationalised approach to controlling the family's assets would be sensible – she should pass her jewels, gold and property deeds to him for his safe management. Elizabeth saw the sense in this suggestion and was quite prepared to sign everything over to her son, until the intervention of the steward of the estate, William Hartgill. The steward suggested that any such arrangement should involve Charles providing an annuity for his mother to live on. Following an ugly and violent row, Charles left the house in an empty-handed rage.

On the following Sunday, twenty of Baron Stourton's henchmen lurked in Kilmington churchyard, awaiting the arrival of William Hartgill and his family. By chance, Hartgill's son John had brought a bow and crossbow to church with him, as he intended to join a hunting party after the service.

As the Hartgills approached, Stourton and his mob drew their swords and attacked. John Hartgill felled one opponent with his bow before the family dashed for the sanctuary of the church and barricaded themselves within the tower. From here they successfully held off the Baron and his cronies until the arrival on the scene of Sir Thomas Speak, the High Sheriff of Somerset.

Stourton was imprisoned and ordered to pay compensation to the Hartgills, although he refused to comply with the latter sentence. Released from gaol in 1555 he returned home, but his grudge against the Hartgills held strong. As Christmas approached, Stourton plotted a new deception. Hoping that the season's moods would provide a cover, he sent word to the Hartgills offering to meet them at Kilmington church, settle the compensation debt and put the feud to rest.

William Hartgill and his family were naturally unconvinced of the Baron's motives and made arrangements to ensure other parties would be at the church at the arranged time, but on the day Stourton presented a purse full of coins and an oath of friendship. However, after the service had ended, the congregation walked out of the church to find they were under the watch of two dozen gunmen hired by Stourton.

With no trace of magnanimity in his moment of triumph, Baron Stourton had William and John Hartgill bound and thrown on to a cart. Mrs Hartgill protested but Stourton himself stabbed her.

The murderous Baron Stourton, hanged in Salisbury in 1557.

The congregation tried to intervene but were overpowered by the heavily armed mercenaries. The cart pulled away and the Hartgill men were gone.

A guilty conscience pricked. A few days after the event the local magistrate, Sir Anthony Hungerford, was visited by one of Stourton's hirelings. The turncoat claimed the baron had originally told the men he intended to kidnap the Hartgills and give them a severe retributive beating, but on arrival at the big house they had been taken on to the terrace and done to death, whilst Stourton watched from a doorway. The man led Hungerford to the bodies before fleeing the area. Baron Stourton and four of his men were arrested that same evening – a search of the Stourton home revealing clear evidence of the murder, stolen livestock and the proceeds of a local robbery.

The four men arrested at the same time as Stourton were hanged at Kilmington, where the churchyard is reputedly haunted by the events of that winter Sunday. William and John Hartgill are often seen walking together as if in serious conference. On occasion they are watched by a man armed with a gun and sword, skulking amongst the trees and shrubbery. The city of Salisbury also has a spectral presence as a result of this tragic episode.

Due to his status, Stourton was taken to London for trial. He was found guilty of murder and returned to Wiltshire for execution of the sentence. On 6 March 1557 he was hanged in the Market Place at Salisbury from where, it has been said, his body was transported to the cathedral for burial.

A phantom silken noose has been seen in Salisbury Cathedral's Trinity Chapel near St Osmund's shrine. (Timezone Collection)

It seems unlikely that a convicted murderer, supposed nobleman or not, would have been allowed to be buried in consecrated ground. Although it has been suggested that a possible location might have been in the doorway of Beauchamp's Chantry, within the thickness of the cathedral wall, but within neither the building nor the grounds.

However, it is certain that the cathedral's Trinity chapel once held a macabre artefact of the hanging. Queen Mary had refused to follow the convention of allowing this 'noble' man to be beheaded instead of hanged, and had ordered he should go to the gallows like any other common criminal. However, his alleged importance of rank was afforded some undeserved significance when, instead of the usual rough hemp, his throat was allowed to be caressed by a cord of the finest silk, to ease his passage into eternity.

The silken noose was suspended in the Trinity chapel for more than 200 years, in two locations: one over the doorway in the south wall of the chapel leading to Beauchamp's Chantry and the other over the remains of St Osmund's shrine. In 1780 the noose was removed on the grounds of bad taste, but its phantom has subsequently often been seen shimmering amongst the building's kaleidoscope of light and half-light.

On the death of Charles Stourton, his titles and estates passed to his eldest son, John, the 9th Baron, who to the relief of all had not inherited his father's worst attributes. Alongside the two aristocrats we have read about, there are stories to be told about those from the lower classes who paid for misdemeanours with their lives – even, in one case, for the misdemeanours of others.

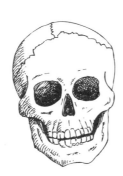

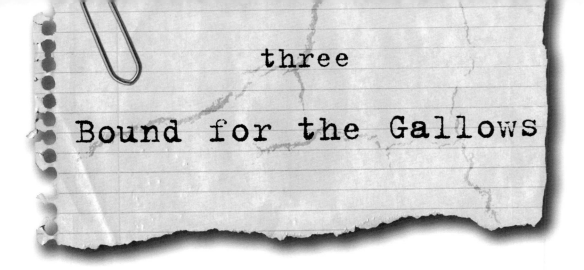

three

Bound for the Gallows

The Odstock Curse and Others who Hanged

Our next story is about a spirit that lived on not as a tormented soul walking the Earth in search of deliverance, but rather in the form of a curse against those who might besmirch his somewhat heroic story. The sequence of events begins to the north-west of Salisbury and ends to the south – with a dramatic centrepiece in the city itself.

In 1801 a horse, the property of John Maish, was stolen at Semington, near Melksham. In April of that year a Gypsy named Joshua Scamp, having been convicted of, and condemned to death for, the crime at the Lent Assizes was led towards a platform constructed at Fisherton, near Salisbury.

Scamp was reported to have ascended the platform with a firm step before looking around the assembled crowd for his family and friends. Catching sight of his wife and daughter, he called them to him and asked if they would be prepared to take his body away. Following their confirmation, Scamp spoke with a number of different persons.

He made a particular statement to one individual, 'You see what you have brought me to. Live soberly and take care of your wife and family'. The language used could be interpreted as evidence of the desperation that had driven the condemned to his crime, but nevertheless he continued to assert his innocence.

Contemporary reports remark that Scamp faced his last moments with 'undaunted courage, unmixed with indecent levity or stupid insensibility'. He stretched the hangman's rope tight with his own hands to try its strength before giving a signal that he was ready. The platform was lowered and Scamp died in a short time.

He was described as being a remarkably strong and robust man. Aged between forty and fifty, he left several children by two wives. His daughter by his first wife, aged about fifteen, had accompanied her stepmother in witnessing the execution and was understandably deeply affected: 'a piercing shriek bespoke her anguish, and much excited the commiseration of the spectators, when he was launched from the platform'. On being released from the noose, Joshua Scamp's body was placed in a plain coffin

The Gypsy Joshua Scamp was hung at Fisherton, Salisbury, in 1801. (Perry Harris)

and conveyed by his family to Odstock, where it was interred at St Mary's church.

Prior to the hanging, the Gypsy community had made considerable efforts to save Scamp from capital punishment. This unusual degree of engagement with the authorities allowed some respite, in as much that he did not hang until a good few weeks after others condemned at the Lent Assizes.

The reason for such intense lobbying on Scamp's behalf became apparent some time later. It transpired that the man he had specifically addressed from the platform at Fisherton was his daughter's husband, and that rather than an obtuse 'confession', the words he had used were a reminder of the need to live a good life in atonement. The son-in-law, himself now condemned

St Mary's church, Odstock, home to the famous Gypsy curse. (Timezone Collection)

to hang for horse theft, confessed from the gallows that Scamp had been hanged an innocent man, wilfully protecting the younger man, who had actually stolen the horse at Semington.

Scamp's sacrifice was remembered by the Gypsies. Each year, on the anniversary of his death, they made the pilgrimage to the churchyard at Odstock. As time passed, the annual event became more raucous until the point where the church authorities, aware of the impending date, decided to lock the church, remove a bench that had been set by Scamp's grave and cut back a briar growing over his resting place.

On discovering these actions the Gypsies are said to have ransacked the church, cut the bell-rope, overturned tombstones and retired to a neighbouring inn where they got unholy drunk. The Gypsy Queen then returned to the churchyard at nightfall and laid a variety of curses. She gave oath that the rector would not be preaching in twelve months' time, that bad luck would haunt the churchwarden Farmer Hodding for two years and that James Hackett, the sexton, would be in the ground before she next returned to Odstock. Two half-Gypsies, who had opposed her people's actions, were promised a 'sudden and quick' death. Then a final curse was laid on the church door: whoever might lock it would lie in their grave within a year.

Sure enough, the rector had a stroke that resulted in a speech impediment leaving him unable to preach, Farmer Hodding went bankrupt and James Hackett died from heart failure while working on the roads. The two cursed half-Gypsies mysteriously disappeared – skeletons were subsequently found in a grave on Odstock Down.

Two men were said to have locked the church door during the early part of the twentieth century, one unknowingly and

The grave of Joshua Scamp in Odstock Graveyard. (Timezone Collection)

one deliberately – both died within twelve months. The key was then thrown into the river Ebble, which jangles through the meadows opposite the church.

In a Britain where the State has not officially killed a criminal in almost half a century, Scamp's execution for horse theft seems exceptionally harsh – notwithstanding his innocence. However, it was by no means unusual in 1801. Twelve men were executed in Salisbury that year – one for murder, one for highway robbery and the other ten for stealing livestock.

As well as Scamp, at the Lent Assizes Judges Sir Alexander Thompson and Sir Simon Le Blanc condemned James Adams for highway robbery and Thomas Elms, Abraham Long, Charles Vincent, Joseph Davis and David Mitchell, all for sheep stealing. These men were hanged on 24 March, apparently all facing their destiny 'in a manner becoming their unhappy situation'!

Twenty-five-year-old Daniel Broom was condemned at the same session, for the murder of Mary Broom, the wife of his brother, at Yatton Keynell near Chippenham. Broom was a common labourer and lodged with his brother and sister-in-law. His motive for killing the unfortunate woman was that the two men might live more, as Daniel put it, 'comfortably'. He felt that Mary was not as good a wife as she should have been and, without provocation, knocked her down and hacked her head off with a hatchet.

It is interesting to compare the language used in contemporary reports of Joshua Scamp's hanging, in which the man's dignity and nobility shine through, with those of Broom's last moments.

The latter man is given no credit:

He appears to have been an exceedingly ignorant man and of very obtuse feeling. He went to his execution as he would have done to any ordinary place of business, without a sigh, without a murmur, or any other token of contrition or emotion. To attempt to create any religious feeling, or render him sensible of the enormity of his sins, was altogether useless. His intellectual calibre being too narrowed to allow him to comprehend any remarks on the subject.

Compared with the lurid tales surrounding Joshua Scamp and Daniel Broom, the hangings arising from the Summer Assizes, at which Judge Le Blanc was joined by Sir Robert Graham, might seem somewhat tame.

Fisherton, near Salisbury, the scene of many hangings.

Following the Assizes, Isaac Box was hanged for stealing a calf at Whitley, near Melksham. The twenty-seven year old confessed to extensive sheep, calf and poultry theft as well as two counts of burglary and one of highway robbery. He also confessed to stealing a silver tankard from a house belonging to a Mr Ferris at Devizes, 'while it was on fire'. He had then sold the tankard for 5 guineas to 'a tradesman of reputable appearance', who had indicated that such items 'were not long in his possession before they were melted'.

John Ockwell and William Bestly, condemned for sheep stealing, were, by comparison, relative innocents. They solemnly declared this to be their first offence and a number of people spoke in their favour at their trial. After being sentenced they appeared resigned and penitent … but there was to be no mercy.

Charles Rudman, another inveterate livestock thief, was hanged for stealing sheep at Bradford-on-Avon, but he may have escaped the greater charge. From comments he made to the turnkey at Fisherton Gaol, he was later suspected of the murder of a servant girl on the road between Chippenham and Corsham. The girl had sold butter at Chippenham market but on her home return was waylaid, robbed of 18s and murdered. The perpetrators of the crime had never been found.

Rudman asked the turnkey if he had heard of the murder. The gaoler invited him to relieve his conscience if he had anything to say in the matter, to which Rudman's only response was, 'he knew who did it, but that it was not committed by him'.

The nineteenth-century equivalent of the chattering classes continued to be as fascinated by the demeanour and behaviour of the condemned after their convictions as by the detail of their crimes. In 1810,

Thomas Jones (alias Hughes) and Richard Francis were hanged for what seems to have been a fairly ordinary jewellery theft in Salisbury.

The caper was enlivened somewhat by the apprehension of the felons by a stagecoach guard en route to London, but it is the day of the hanging that is reported most vividly. Francis' conduct was 'exemplary and devout', but that of Jones (an escaped convict) was 'very indifferent, even to the last moment'. At the foot of the platform, Jones was greeted with a wish that he might seek the forgiveness of his Maker, to which 'he replied coolly "Thank You" in about the same manner as he would have done to a common salutation'. Once the noose was around his neck, Jones looked casually around and threw his hat to the crowd. Owing to displacement of the rope and his light weight, Jones died with 'much protracted suffering' – to the evident satisfaction of the writer.

Henry Wynn, hanged in 1836 for the murder of Eliza Jones at Highworth, was reported as being 'a mean looking little man, with a vulgar, un-intellectual countenance'. He is, however, given some credit for becoming penitent whilst in prison, confessing that his life had been one 'of such hardened sin that he feared God would never take heed of his prayers for forgiveness'.

Wynn walked to the scaffold with 'much firmness, united in the last prayers with that kind of composure in which he would perform any common act of duty'. He requested that the hangman remove his cravat and the executioner did so, placing the item in the breast pocket of the condemned. Wynn indicated this was pointless, as he would have no more use for it. Then, asking that everything might be 'expeditiously managed', he mounted the platform, threw the cravat to the crowd and, 'having ejaculated a few words, ceased to exist'.

Wynn was interred within the walls of Fisherton Gaol – in the first-class misdemeanant's yard. Previously, the bodies of executed murderers had generally been given to the prison surgeon for the purposes of dissection, although some of those not taken away by relatives or friends of the deceased were interred in St Clement's churchyard in Fisherton. The execution of Wynn was the first to take place in Salisbury following an Act of Parliament that decreed remains of the executed were to be buried within the precincts of the prison in which they were last confined.

Although the gallows used to dispatch Wynn were sited at the long-standing place of execution at the junction of Wilton Road with Devizes Road, his final resting place was in fact the second Fisherton Gaol.

In 1808 it was decided that the old county gaol, near Fisherton Bridge, was unhealthy and at risk of flooding because of its close proximity to the river Avon, and it was decided that it should be closed. A site was chosen for a new gaol between Turnpike Lane (now St Paul's Road) and the southern end of Devizes Road. At the time the later intervening Sidney Street and York Road had not been built and the area – nowadays dominated by the St Paul's roundabout – was very much at the edge of town.

Work started on the new gaol in 1818 and it was first occupied in August 1822. The building work – carried out by Salisbury contractor John Peniston under the guidance of Mr T. Hopper, architect – cost a total of £40,000 and every one of the bricks used was a 'Fisherton', made on the spot from the clay that was dug out.

The new gaol was hailed as a great advance. The *Salisbury & Winchester Journal* commented that:

The general intercourse of prisoners, whereby the more abandoned are able to instruct the youth just launched into vice, in every species of depravation, is an evil which has been long felt. Our gaols have hitherto tended rather to confirm the prisoner in the habits of wickedness than to amend his morals. The present plan will unite the desired purpose of a reformatory with a place of confinement; every prisoner will be compelled to spend his hours in solitude; personal access of any but his keeper will no longer be suffered, and his diet must be of the 'simplest kind, bread and water ...' The female prisoners are to be divided from the men and to be treated in like manner.

The gaol contained ninety-six cells with seven courtyards, including two for female prisoners. At the centre were the governor's and matron's quarters, a chapel and an enclosure for female debtors. The average occupancy was approximately two-thirds of the overall maximum, with the number of committals usually fluctuating between 300 and 400 per year. A large percentage of the inmates were being remanded in custody, pending the six-monthly Assizes.

The gate house was on the Devizes Road. Behind this was the governor's house, to each side of which were rows of dank cells below ground level. These passed under what is now York Road on one side and halfway to St Paul's Road on the other. A similar row of cells was constructed behind the house, and behind this was the chapel.

Although the use of the gaol ceased in 1870 and much of the original structure was demolished in 1875, a *Salisbury Journal* reporter was allowed to inspect the site in 1958. The cells that then remained were damp, cramped – around 8ft x 6ft – and with a brick-vaulted roof barely 6ft high.

The new Fisherton Gaol contained rows of dank cells, below ground level. (George Cruikshank)

The vaulted passageway was twice the width of the cells themselves. Access to each cell was through a small opening and, except perhaps for that gleaned from candles in the passage, the inmates would only have seen light when allowed into the yard for exercising. There was no evidence of any provision for heating. The debtors' accommodation appeared to have been a single large, open room. The old chapel remained in good repair – including the gallery probably used by priests to address the wretched congregation below.

A total of seventy-one executions took place at Fisherton between 1801 and 1850, twelve of which, as we have already seen, were in the first year of that period. In many of the latter years there were no executions here at all – the last execution was in 1855. The condemned man was William Wright, who had been found guilty of the murder of Ann Collins at Lydiard Tregoze, near Swindon.

The scaffold was erected early on a Tuesday morning, and shortly before 11 a.m. the chaplain met with Wright in the prison chapel and urged him to use his last few moments wisely. The Holy Sacrament was then administered, and at 11.40 a.m. the murderer, accompanied by the under-sheriff and others, proceeded to the gallows whilst the chaplain read the burial service.

Wright appeared deeply affected, sobbed violently and prayed earnestly. He took his leave of the governor and shook hands with the chaplain and the under-sheriff, before Calcraft, the executioner, proceeded to pinion him. Wright had expressed a wish to address the crowd, but now declined to do so. The procession ascended the steps to the scaffold. The condemned's firmness held as he moved beneath the beam, the rope was placed round his neck and adjusted, and the cap drawn over his eyes.

The chaplain proceeded with his solemn service and at a given signal the bolt was drawn, and the unfortunate man was launched into eternity. Wright's death was almost instantaneous and his fall from 'The Drop' caused a wound inflicted at the time of the murder to break out afresh, serving only to increase the horror of the spectacle.

In a 1919 *Salisbury Times* article, a Mr Robert Harding – 'possibly the oldest resident in Fisherton' – recalled how as a boy he would be woken during the night by the noise of workmen erecting the gallows. He also spoke of the ceremony of these occasions: the procession from the gaol, the adjusting of the rope around the neck, the black hood, the reading of the burial service ... the drawing of the bolt ...

Executions were certainly a big draw: there was an estimated crowd of 15,000 at the hanging of Robert Watkins for murder in 1819, and a not quite so impressive 10,000 for that of George Maslen, hanged for attempted murder in 1838. Whilst it had risen to more than 11,000 by the latter date, at the time of the earlier, larger event the combined population of Salisbury and Fisherton Anger was a little over 9,000.

In 1866 a Royal Commission recommended the abolition of public executions and William Wright's hanging proved to be the last in Salisbury – public or otherwise. Fisherton gaol closed in 1870 and the six-acre site was later put up for sale. It was purchased in 1875 by Thomas Leach, a grocer who owned a shop in the Market Place, and Thomas Scammell, who had a business in Fisherton Street.

Most of the buildings were demolished, but not before the site was opened for a public viewing on 1 July 1875. Nearly 2,000 curious citizens paid a total of £19 8s 10d (which was donated to the St Paul's church enlargement fund) for the privilege of inspecting the premises and listening to gospel addresses in the garden and a sermon in the chapel.

Following some demolition work, the gaol building was renamed Radnor House and became a school for girls, operated by the Misses Harding, where 'a limited number of young ladies' were educated at a cost of 35 to 45 guineas per annum. The prospectus promised that each pupil would have a bed and advised they 'should bring two forks, a dessert spoon and tea spoon, four dinner napkins and six towels'.

Mr E.O. Harding, a relative of the school proprietors, recalled how evidence remained of the somewhat less luxurious lifestyle of former occupants:

An uncle used to take me down to see the cells and used to scare the life out of me. At that time there were still marks on the ceilings of the cells where the prisoners had used candle smoke to make drawings. There was a moon and a sun among other things and I can only think they had something to do with their misery.

Part of the Fisherton Gaol building was renamed Radnor House. The whole site of Fisherton Gaol was finally demolished in 1969. (Timezone collection)

By 1905, St Paul's Road, York Road, Sidney Street, George Street and Meadow Road had been built across parts of the site. Radnor House was by now owned by Dr Corbin Finch and leased to the War Department for use as an office for HQ Southern Command. In 1913 the remainder of the gaol grounds were also leased to the War Department by a Mrs Baskin. Huts were built on the site in 1914, and in May 1922 the freehold of the site passed from Mrs Baskin to the War Department.

In May 1940 the site was found to be too cramped and HQ Southern Command relocated to Wilton House. However, some ancillary services remained at Radnor House into the 1950s and, during the Second World War, Salisbury's No. 1 Auxiliary Fire Station was set up at a former Wall's ice-cream depot in Devizes Road, on the site of part of the old gaol grounds.

The entire site was finally cleared in 1969 in preparation for the construction of Salisbury's relief road, now known as Churchill Way, one end of which is at the St Paul's roundabout, constructed across part of the old gaol grounds.

Georgian and Victorian gaol conditions and methods of punishment appear brutal to modern sensitivities, but they were quite an improvement on the old Fisherton Gaol, where the subjects of our next chapter had been interred.

The streets around the area have their own ghost stories – we will read in later chapters about a suicidal entrepreneur, a murdered schoolboy and the question of whether or not the old gallows site is cursed. There is little doubt that the old prison site itself – still referred to as 'the gaolyards' by local people, even those born long after its closure – retains an indeterminate atmosphere.

Those who attended the old, now demolished, St Paul's school recall being able to peer in to pavement level openings of the old gaol buildings, and scaring one another with what they imagined they had seen in the murk.

The underpasses connecting Fisherton Street, Wilton Road and Devizes Road with York Road are at the same level as some of the old cells once were. The walls of the underpasses have a particularly cold and damp feel – especially those in the tunnel leading to York Road, which also seems somehow noiseless compared to others around the city. If it were not for the excavations needed to accommodate the roundabout and its infrastructure, would those who had spent such a wretched time in the confines of Fisherton Gaol now be content to rest easy and not make themselves known to passing pedestrians?

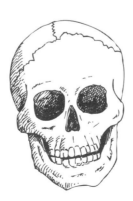

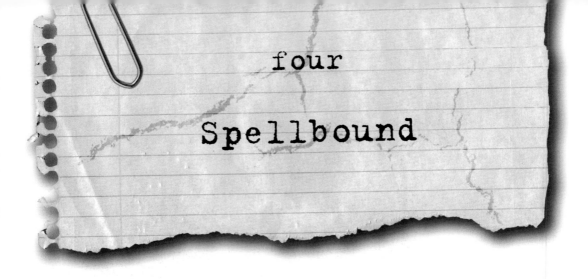

four

Spellbound

The Sarum Witch Trials

In 1568 Salisbury's Justices of the Peace decided to build a gaol. The first proposed site was at East Harnham, in full view of the Bishop's Palace. Bishop Jewell was not enamoured by the idea and wrote to the Justices to say so: 'it will be sutche annoiance unto me, beinge placed within one flighte shoote of my house, and directly before my studie and chamber windowe'. The plan was abandoned and the bishop offered to, 'deale for another place in fishertone'. Work was started on the new gaol in 1569, on a site where today stands the clock tower near Fisherton Bridge.

The building comprised two storeys and measured 53ft by 29ft, with an adjoining woman's prison and keeper's house. The gaol walls were 23ft in height. The inner walls were built in burr-stone and there were seven windows, each of 3ft by 2ft in size. The iron bars of each window weighed 21lb, at a cost of 3d for 1lb, the internal iron grating weighed 254lb. Prisoners were issued with a single blanket once every eight weeks – but were never bathed unless the gaol's surgeon specifically requested so.

The burr-stone – eighty loads at 8d each – had been plundered from the abandoned castle at Old Sarum, but not until labourers had toiled for twelve days to build a road good enough for the carts to carry it. Progress was slow as there was difficulty in securing funding – rate paying was then a new concept. The gaol was not completed until 1578, at a total cost of £896 3s 7½d.

Improvements carried out in 1783 saw each prisoner provided with an individual cell measuring 8ft by 10ft 6in, with windows of double-iron gratings. In total, twenty-four cells were accommodated on three storeys. In 1790 the Justices obtained a machine for the purposes of public executions and launched it with a triple hanging. The machine was apparently 'so elevated that the spectacle may be seen from the street before the gates of the gaol'.

As well as the machine, the gallows at the junction of Wilton Road with Devizes Road were also used to dispatch the condemned inmates of the old Fisherton Gaol. Having been taken in an open cart to the junction, each prisoner had a rope tied around their neck and the cart was drawn up under the gallows. The rope was then tied

The clock tower near Fisherton Bridge where work was started on the new gaol in 1569. (Timezone Collection)

to the cross beam and the horses whipped to pull the cart away, leaving the offenders choking and kicking the air in vain.

One of the poor unfortunates who made this final journey was Anne Bodenham, a Fisherton woman found guilty of witchcraft in a sensational trial of 1653. During Henry VIII's reign witchcraft was declared a felony, but this was later repealed. The status of felony was reintroduced under Elizabeth, with the new bill containing severe penalties for sorcery and witchcraft.

The case of Anne Bodenham was recorded contemporarily by an Edmond Bower of Shaftesbury. His full account was entitled 'Dr Lamb Revived – witchcraft condemned in Anne Bodenham' with a shorter, perhaps tabloid-style version made available as 'Dr Lamb's Darling ... or Strange and Terrible News from Salisbury'.

Dr Lamb was an infamous astrologer, practitioner of magic and untrained 'doctor' with an influence in court though the patronage of the Duke of Buckingham.

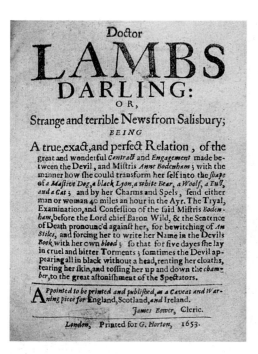

Doctor

LAMBS

DARLING:

OR,

Strange and terrible News from Salisbury;

BEING

A true, exact, and perfect Relation, of the great and wonderful *Contract* and *Engagement* made between the Devil, and Miſtris *Anne Bodenham*; with the manner how ſhe could transform her ſelf into the *ſhape* of a *Maſtive Dog*, a black *Lyon*, a *white Bear*, a *Wolf*, a *Bull*, and a *Cat*; and by her Charms and Spels, ſend either man or woman 40 miles an hour in the Ayr. The Tryal, Examination, and Confeſſion of the ſaid Miſtris *Bodenham*, before the Lord chief Baron Wild, & the Sentence of Death pronounc'd againſt her, for bewitching of *An Stiles*, and forcing her to write her Name in the Devils *Book* with her own *blood*; ſo that for five dayes ſhe lay in cruel and bitter Torments; ſomtimes the Devil appearing all in black without a head, renting her cloaths, tearing her ſkin, and toſſing her up and down the *chamber*, to the great aſtoniſhment of the Spectators.

Appointed to be printed and publiſhed, as a Caveat and Warning piece for England, Scotland, and Ireland.

James Bower, Cleric.

London, Printed for *G. Horton*, 1653.

The case of Anne Bodenham of Fisherton was recorded in the publication Dr Lamb's Darling.

Despite his connections, Lamb stood trial for invoking evil spirits and the rape of an eleven-year-old girl. He was pardoned for the latter but met his death in London in 1628, at the hands of a mob that believed the charge and despised his corrupt and evil influence.

One of Dr Lamb's many clients had sent her servant, Anne Bodenham, to act as a go-between in a particular case. Bodenham was impressed by Lamb's talents, became his servant and in turn acquired her own knowledge of his arts.

Bodenham later married a clothier from Fisherton, near Salisbury, and worked there herself as a 'cunning woman'. Her services including teaching children to read, recovering lost items and curing sickness. She was very successful, claiming to have 'gotten many a penny and done hundreds of people good'. The association with Dr Lamb no doubt enhanced Bodenham's

reputation and, in this superstitious age, the trade of purveying magic could be seen as reputable by the upper classes — whatever its legal status.

The sequence of events that led to her downfall started with the loss — or possible theft — of a silver spoon at the home of a Mr Goddard in The Close, which he shared, somewhat uncomfortably, with his extended family. A servant girl named Anne Styles was sent to Anne Bodenham's house in Fisherton for help — the spoon was not found but Bodenham still demanded payment of a shilling and a pot of beer.

On her return to her Master's house, Styles was asked by Goddard's son-in-law Mason to go back to the cunning woman to ask about three gold coins he had lost. This time Bodenham demanded 7s and then 'opened three Books, in which there seemed to be severall pictures, and amongst the rest the picture of the Devill … with his Cloven feet and Claws'.

Anne Styles was invited to look into a green scrying glass placed on one of the books, where she saw 'the shape of many persons, and what they were doing of in her Master's house' — 'scrying' being a magical practice by which things could be physically seen from elsewhere. In a separate event, later that day, Mrs Goddard became concerned, having borrowed money from her daughter-in-law. The coins were stained black and Mrs Goddard believed this was an attempt at poisoning.

Mrs Goddard sent Anne back to the witch for advice and on this occasion the girl was guided over Crane Street Bridge by a strange black dog. Anne Bodenham promised to prevent the poisoning for a fee of 5s. The following day Styles was sent to Fisherton again, where it was foretold that the poisoning was planned for Friday … but would be prevented.

Anne Bodenham was found guilty of witchcraft in the sensational trial of 1653. (Perry Harris)

Later that same day, the Goddards' son-in-law, Mason, sent Styles to obtain protection for him from a gambling crony – she returned with a cross-shaped paper amulet containing yellow powder.

Mason was impressed and sent her back to Bodenham for advice on a law suit between himself and Goddard.

On this occasion Anne Bodenham began to demonstrate the full range of her professional expertise. She drew a circle on the floor with a staff and 'placed in the Circle an earthen pan of Coles. Wherein she threw something, which burning caused a noysome stinck'. The witch invoked the Devil, whereupon five ragged spirits appeared and then vanished. Bodenham advised that Mason should demand a £1,500 lump sum plus £500 per annum from his father-in-law, Goddard. If this was refused the law suit should be pursued.

The matter of Mrs Goddard's impending poisoning was still to be resolved. Anne Styles was sent by Bodenham to buy arsenic, which would be mystically burned as a preventative. Styles visited the witch again over subsequent days and twice witnessed her displaying diabolical pictures, calling on the Devil to conjure up more evil spirits – and using the scrying glass to find arsenic hidden under Sarah Goddard's bed.

The spirits took Anne Styles to a meadow near Wilton to pick vervine and dill. These herbs, together with Anne Bodenham's own nail parings, were to be used in potions to be administered in the drink or broth of the cursed – in this case the Goddard's daughters-in-law – 'to rot their Guts in their Bellies;…to make their Teeth fall out of their Heads;…to make them drunk and mad'. For the potion to be effective it was necessary for the dispenser to cross themselves in the name of Jesus and say the Creed backwards and forwards.

The Goddards' daughters-in-law had become suspicious of Styles' visits to the witch. They made enquiries of the Salisbury apothecaries and found that the servant had bought arsenic. The Goddard household became anxious that their complicity with the supernatural might be brought to light and the girl was dismissed.

Before leaving Salisbury, Anne Styles made a further visit to Anne Bodenham, who invited her to stay so that she could teach her 'to doe as she did and that she should ever be taken'. The girl declined so Bodenham made her take a vow of silence – signed in her own blood in the witch's book of the Devil. Styles then fled for London, but she was overtaken by Master Chandler (another of the Goddards' sons-in-law). It was during the return journey that she confessed all before falling into a coma, racked with terrible convulsions.

Having been examined by the magistrate, Edward Tucker, Styles and Bodenham were committed to Fisherton Gaol on a charge of attempted poisoning. Edmond Bower and his friends visited the gaol, where they saw Styles fitting so powerfully that it needed six men to restrain her:

> … for five dayes she lay in cruel and bitter Torments; sometimes the Devil appearing all in black without a head, renting her cloaths, tearing her skin, and tossing her up and down the chamber, to the great astonishment of the Spectators.

The visitors also met with Anne Bodenham and quizzed her about her religion; they encouraged her to seek salvation through prayer. Bower remembered reading advice suggesting bringing a bewitched person into the presence of the bewitcher. This was achieved, and the fits duly transferred to the witch as Anne Styles recovered. In his interviews with her, Bower discovered that Bodenham, 'could transform her self into any shape of a Mastive Dog, a black Lyon, a white Bear, a Woolf, a Bull and a Cat, and by her Charms and Spels, send either man or woman 40 miles a hour in the Ayr'.

Anne Bodenham was tried at the Lent Assizes, found guilty of witchcraft and condemned to death. She refused to admit her guilt, despite the discovery that her body of the great Jehovah of Heaven, to restore her to her former state and condition, crying out, *Oh what a loving God have I to break me off with this league from the Devil! Oh what a sweet Saviour have I that hath ransom'd my poor soul from the infernal Lake, & brought me even from the very brinks of Hell: Blessed be his name; he hath wrought my deliverance, and dispossessed the evil spirit.* Many other strange and diabolical actions, the foresaid Witch bothpractised and put in execution; namely, by her several Charms and Spels, she would convey either man or woman 40 miles an hour in the Air, she was one that would undertake to cure almost any Diseases by the said Charms, but somtimes used physical ingredients, to cure her abominable practices; she would undertake to procure things that were lost, and restore goods that were stoln; she could transform her self into any shape whatsoever, *viz.*

A Mastive Dog,
A black Lyon,
A white Bear,
A Woolf,
A Monkey,
A Horse,
A Bull,
And a Calf.

*A page from the publication on Anne Bodenham,
Dr Lamb's Darling.*

showed the marks of a witch. She would not pray — or be prayed for — and refused to reveal the whereabouts of her magic book or of other witches in the area.

Whilst in gaol, the witch had asked to be buried under the gallows. On the day of her execution she was taken from the gaol; she begged for beer at every house along the route to her place of execution. Edmond Bower reported that in her last days she was, 'desirous for drink, and had not Mr Undersheriffs prudence been such as to restrain her from it, she would have died drunk'.

At the gallows, Bower again tried to persuade Bodenham to confess. She offered to reveal the location of £1,000 hidden in the Earl of Pembroke's garden in return for her freedom before requesting a knife to 'run it into her heart-blood'. The executioner prevented the witch from prematurely leaping from the gallows, and then asked for her forgiveness: 'Forgive thee? A pox on thee, turn me off; which were the last words she spake'.

Despite possible modern perceptions, witch trials were not that common. Certainly others held in Salisbury were not as well as documented as the Bodenham case, if at all.

In 1565 Agnes, widow of Stanley Mylles, became involved in a feud over an inheritance. Mylles was condemned and hanged at Fisherton for the murder, by witchcraft, of William Baynton, the infant son and heir apparent of Edward and Agnes Baynton. The case was proved by the Somerset witchfinder Jane Marshe, who claimed that Mylles had been 'inticed and procured' by the Bayntons' sister-in-law Dorothy, to whose sons the disputed estate would now pass.

Dorothy Baynton then brought a case of false accusation against Jane Marshe, on the grounds that Agnes Baynton had procured Mylles and then paid Marshe to implicate Dorothy. Bishop Jewell believed this version of events and Jane Marshe was kept in Fisherton Gaol for six months. Having been told she would 'lie, rot and consume' in gaol, she changed her story to gain freedom.

Ninety years later, Margery Gyngell was condemned to death for bewitching Eleanor Lyddiard 'to death' and Anne Beedle 'so that she pined and lamed'. She was hanged on 3 May 1655, at the same time as the seven Salisbury victims of the failed Royalist 'Rising in the West'.

In 1659 a widow named Orchard requested yeast from the daughter of Hugh Bartholomew of Malmesbury. On refusal of the request, the widow went away muttering, and a large chest in the room above 'was lifted up and let fall so that it shook the whole house'. The chest contained £200 and the 'gingling' of the money could be heard. Bartholomew chased the widow and made accusations towards her, to which she replied, 'You lie, you old Rogue; your chest is not broken, the nayles are only drawn and there is never a penny of your money gone', which proved to be true.

Some months later Widow Orchard asked the daughter of a Burbage gardener for food. The girl was tired from pulling up and washing carrots and said she must wash, as her hands were sandy, and eat first herself. On this, Widow Orchard trotted three times around the garden and squatted down, whilst muttering unintelligible words.

Once the widow had left the scene, the girl washed her hands in the water, with the result that, 'her fingers were distorted in their joyntes, one this way, another that way,

and with such extreme torment, that she cryed out as if one had been about to kill her ... and say'd that wicked old woman had bewitched her'.

Widow Orchard was caught three days later in Edington and brought back to Burbage, where the girl was sleepless with pain and fever. The old woman claimed that the girl must have washed her hands in unclean water as she had not bewitched her. Widow Orchard asked to see the same water, dipped her finger into it and described three circles, 'contrary to the course of the Sun'. The girl

Salisbury's Protestant martyrs were burnt at the stake in 1556.

then dipped her own hands back into the water and, 'the pain and distortion ceased but her fingers were left without strength'. Consequently, the widow was taken to the gaol in Salisbury, where she was later executed following a conviction for witchcraft.

There is no doubt that there was a religious element to the pursuit and conviction of these 'cunning women', and another sequence of events with a horrific ending came about as a direct result of State-sponsored bigotry.

John Maundrel was a Protestant, the son of a farmer from Rowde, near Devizes, who himself lived in nearby Keevil. Although unable to read, Maundrel carried the New Testament at all times in order that it could always be read to him – in any case his memory was that good that he could recite most of the book by heart.

Maundrel was first punished for having spoken against the use of holy water and bread at Edington Abbey by being made to wear a white sheet and carry a candle in the market place in Devizes. Undaunted, he later went to Keevil, along with John Spicer, a freemason, and William Coberly, a tailor, to demonstrate against 'idols' during a church procession. By order of the vicar the three men were placed in the stocks, then brought before a Justice of the Peace and sent to Salisbury, where they were placed before Bishop Capon and Geffrey, the Chancellor of the Diocese.

Following a period of imprisonment the three men were examined as to their beliefs at St Clement's church in Fisherton. They affirmed their faith in the Creed and the scriptures, 'from the first of Genesis to the last of the Apocalypse'. However, they refused to acknowledge the Pope's authority, saying that, 'the Popish Masse was abominable Idolatrie', with Maundrel adding that,

'wooden Images were good to rost a shoulder of mutton, but evill in the Church'.

Chancellor Geffrey condemned the men to death and delivered them to the Sheriff on 24 March 1556. They were taken to a place between Salisbury and Wilton:

> ... where were two postes set for them to be burnt at. Which men comming to the place, they kneeled down and made their prayers secretly together, and then being disclothed to their shirts, John Maundrel spake with a loud voice, not for all Salisbury, which words men judged to be an answer to the Sheriff, which offered the Queene's pardon if he would recant, and after that in like manner spake John Spicer, saying, this is the joyfullest day that ever I saw. Thus were they 3 burnt at two stakes where most constantly they gave their bodies to the fire, and their soules to the Lord for testimonie of his Truth.

John Maundrel was later commemorated by the Maundrel Hall in Fisherton Street, opposite the site of the old gaol where he and his colleagues had been held. The hall has since been replaced by the building that now houses the Slug & Lettuce public house. This is perhaps unfortunate, but the names of Salisbury's Protestant Martyrs are now remembered by a plaque on the outer wall of Malmesbury House, near to St Ann's Gate in The Close.

As we have previously seen, a new Fisherton Gaol was opened in 1822 – replacing that in which our witches and martyrs had been interred. Despite the condemnation of the old gaol for fear of flood and disease, the authorities of the nearby Salisbury Infirmary purchased the buildings and decided to convert the old Governor's house into two wards.

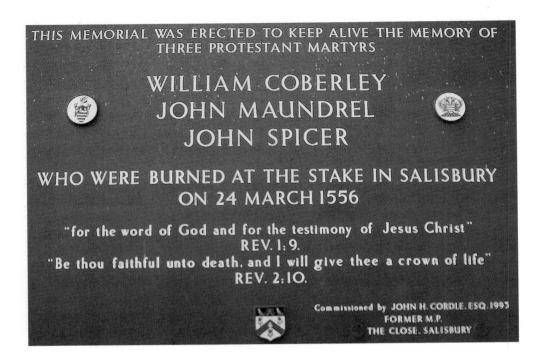

THIS MEMORIAL WAS ERECTED TO KEEP ALIVE THE MEMORY OF
THREE PROTESTANT MARTYRS

WILLIAM COBERLEY
JOHN MAUNDREL
JOHN SPICER

WHO WERE BURNED AT THE STAKE IN SALISBURY
ON 24 MARCH 1556

"for the word of God and for the testimony of Jesus Christ"
REV. 1: 9.
"Be thou faithful unto death, and I will give thee a crown of life"
REV. 2: 10.

Commissioned by JOHN H. CORDLE. ESQ. 1993
FORMER M.P.
THE CLOSE. SALISBURY

The Maundrel plaque in memory of the three martyrs. (Timezone Collection)

However, by 1841 the old prison building was overrun with rats, so they were demolished to make way for a new wing of the hospital. The infirmary was later haunted by the ghost of a matronly looking woman whose walking ghost was split between two floors – the top half passing through one ward and the legs through that below – perhaps because she had died here in an older building, which had different floor levels to those of the new one.

John Roberts MD, of The Close Gate, High Street, Salisbury, was a consulting physician to Salisbury Infirmary from 1854 to 1874. He was also founder of the Salisbury & South Wilts Provident Dispensary and donor of the Roberts Hall in the Salisbury School of Art in New Street.

In 1892 the hospital governors agreed to sell a small part of the infirmary site, where the old gaol had stood, for an illuminated clock tower to be built by Dr Roberts for the benefit of the city, in memory of his first wife, Arabella. An area of approximately 20 sq.ft was sold to Dr Roberts for the sum of £5, and the clock tower was completed in 1893.

The clock tower retains clues to the former use of the site that, although quite hidden and subtle, somehow convey the awful squalor and desolation that must have been felt by the old inmates: two barred windows, now blocked in, survive from the old gaol, because the stretch of wall containing them was used in the base for the clock tower – and a plaque set in the wall is carved with gyves, an old type of fetters or shackles.

At various times there were other sites and methods of capital punishment in Salisbury. The city authorities acquired the freehold of the Greencroft in the mid-sixteenth century. As well as letting the area for recreational use, the city also used it as a burial ground for plague victims and as a place of execution. In March 1772 a Welshman, William Leach,

The carved shackles at the base of the Salisbury clock tower. (Timezone Collection)

was shot here, having been convicted of deserting his regiment.

A pillory and stocks stood in the Market Place until 1837 and 1858 respectively. It was not unusual for those convicted to be bombarded with rotten eggs, vegetables and any other missiles that came to hand, to the extent that they were often maimed or even killed. The last offender to be confined to the stocks was John Selloway on a charge of drunkenness. This was the eighth such charge against him in a period of fourteen months and he was ordered to pay 5s, the default which meant being placed in the stocks for six hours. He was unwilling – or unable – to pay the fine.

A large residential property, Portland House, was later built at the junction of Devizes Road and Wilton Road (where the city gallows had stood) but by the 1930s a fabulous Art Deco garage and filling station, operated by Wessex Motors, was located here. Wessex Motors were a successful firm with a number of premises around the town, specialising in the Morris, Wolseley and Bentley marques.

Alongside the remains of Anne Bodenham, the unhallowed ground of the crossroads became the last resting place of many, whose confused choice of direction in the mortal phase of their existence had led them to the gallows pole. In October 1851 workmen laying a gas main unearthed a number of skeletons, believed to be those of the executed.

The Wessex Motors buildings were later replaced with modern buildings but these have, in turn, been demolished and the junction has now stood vacant and boarded up for many years. Have the ghosts of those hanged at Fisherton cursed the city that killed them by ensuring this prominent, potential landmark site remains a perpetual eyesore?

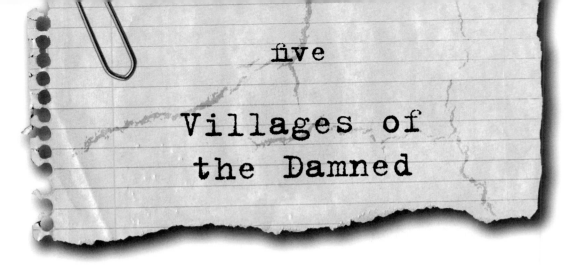

five

Villages of
the Damned

Salisbury's Haunted Hinterland

Many of the villages around Salisbury have their own ghosts, and place names often betray a grisly history. At the edge of the wild expanses of Salisbury Plain, The Gibbet lies just north of Shrewton, where a lane leads off the Devizes Road towards Orcheston. Further along the Devizes Road, at Gore Cross, the Robber's Stone can be found, close to the turning that leads to the ghost village of Imber.

The Robber's Stone was, 'erected by public subscription as a warning to those who presumptuously think to escape the punishment God has threatened against thieves and robbers'. The little monument tells of how, on this very spot, a Mr Dean of Imber was attacked and robbed by four highwaymen on 21 October 1839. After a 'spirited' pursuit lasting three hours, one of the felons – Benjamin Colclough – fell dead on Chitterne Down. The other three – Thomas Saunders, George Waters and Richard Harris – were eventually captured, convicted at the ensuing Quarterly Sessions at Devizes and condemned to transportation for fifteen years.

The burial register at Maddington, near Shrewton, contains the following entry: 'William Lawne, sonne off Giles Lawne barbarously slaine neere the Windemill, Sept 23rd, and buryed the 24th of the same, 1666'. William Lawne had made a large sum of money at market in Warminster. An ostler at the inn where he was staying learned of this and followed him out of the town before shooting him at the spot now known as The Gibbet. The murderer was arrested and hanged in chains on the spot, and local legend has it that nothing would grow on the site. Presumably Lawne's killer spent the end of his mortal existence in the Blind House at Shrewton – an even smaller, damper, airless and darker place of incarceration than the cells of Fisherton Gaol.

Between 1806 and 1824, six men were hanged at Fisherton for highway robbery. The loneliness of the Plain, with routes from London to the west and south-west running across it, was the perfect setting for the highwayman to ply his trade.

The notion of the 'The Highwayman' became a romantic legend and, indeed, many of the more successful practitioners became heroes, or anti-heroes,

AT THIS SPOT
Mr DEAN of Imber was
Attacked and Robbed by
Four Highwaymen in the
evening of Octr 21 1839/
After a spirited pursuit of
three hours one of the Felons
BENJAMIN COLCLOUGH
fell Dead on Chitterne Down.
THOMAS SAUNDERS.
GEORGE WATERS, &
RICHARD HARRIS.
were eventually Captured
and were convicted at the
ensuing Quarter Sessions at
Devizes and Transported for
the term of Fifteen Years.
This Monument is erected
by Public Subscription
as a warning to those who
presumptuously think to
escape the punishment God
has threatened against
Theives and Robbers,

The Robber's Stone near the ghost village of Imber. (Wilfred Chaplin)

Wiltshire highwaymen Thomas Boulter who was hanged at Winchester in 1778. (Mill Farm)

during their own lifetimes and were celebrated in popular literature. In some cases the romanticising could be justified as some highwaymen lived up to the popular image of fearless, carefree, chivalrous, rogues ... men of good breeding fallen on hard times ... gentlemen of the road. However, many were desperate, ruthless thugs, with no regard for their victims or the consequences of their actions.

Almost as much as hanging, the highwayman feared the fate of gibbeting, wherein his executed body would be hung in irons, for as long as it took to rot, in a desolate spot by the side of road – presumably *pour encourager les autres*. The superstitious would often remove parts of the decomposing body – the hair and teeth would be used in potions and remedies, and the hands were particularly favoured for creating 'hands of glory'

(as discussed in Chapter 1). The body could be further mutilated by the weather, the humble maggot and the black-faced crows that inhabited the Plain, and there was little hope that it would ever find its way into consecrated ground. In 1783, the *Salisbury Journal* described the gibbet as, 'a dreadful memento to youth, how they swerve from the paths of rectitude, and transgress the laws of their country'.

Among the highwaymen who worked the Plain was a man named Biss, who was hanged in Salisbury in 1695 and was one of many said to have been a 'Robin Hood' figure from a good background. William Davis – 'The Golden Farmer' – had a remarkable career of almost forty years robbing travellers on the old Exeter Road, before being hanged at Tyburn in 1689, having shot a Salisbury butcher.

Probably the most famous of all Wiltshire highwaymen was Thomas Boulter, the son of a miller from Poulshot, near Devizes, who was hanged at Winchester in 1778 at the age of thirty. He was a heroic character of striking appearance, with fair hair, a good figure, clothes by the best tailors, the best weapons and good manners. He had a horse named Back Bess, just like Dick Turpin.

Out on a lonely stretch of the London Road, the tiny village of Jack's Bush is said to be named after the hiding place of a highwayman. Further north, at the edge of the Wallops, the point where the main road is crossed with that running from Romsey to Tidworth, is known as Leonard's Corner.

A one-time landlord of the Five Bells at Nether Wallop, named Leonard, is said to have committed suicide. At that time this was an act deemed so terrible a sin that the departed could not be buried in consecrated ground. It was the practice that the bodies of suicide victims should be buried at a crossroads and, in this case, it is believed that the poor publican was interred at the spot that still bears his name.

Closer to Salisbury on the same road, Lopcombe ('formerly Lobscombe') Corner was previously known as the 'Golden Balls' owing to the two metal spheres attached to a wooden post which stood at the junction where the Salisbury Road splits to head for Andover and Stockbridge. This artefact was once a gate post to the junction toll house – a replica has recently been erected.

Across the army ranges, in the Bourne Valley, we find the ghosts of two clergymen. The one-time curate of the village of Allington was one evening invited for dinner at the local manor. According to the other diners, the curate over-indulged somewhat and left the house in such a drunken state that he found it difficult to mount his horse; the animal then arrived back at the curate's house without his master.

Rumours of a dark deed began to take hold locally when other villagers noticed that the witnesses to the portentous dinner were behaving secretly and strangely – and then the ghost of the curate began to appear, leading to more excited gossip. The ghost would walk – not ride – from the manor house to the site where the curate's body had been discovered. A few months later, one of the dinner guests was near to death himself and called for a vicar, having the apparent desire to confess a great sin. By the time the vicar reached the bedside, the dying man was unable to speak and passed without revealing the source of his distress.

In 1896, in nearby Cholderton, a clergyman visiting Cholderton House went missing during the night. His dressing gown had also disappeared but his day clothes, money and travelling bag remained in the room. A few days later, the man's body was found at the base of a disused well, near St Nicholas' church, after a passer-by noticed a pair of slippers sitting neatly on the parapet wall.

The coroner recorded an 'Open' verdict. There was no sign of any foul play and it was generally assumed to have been a case of suicide – although there was apparently no obvious reason behind this. It seems, however, that the dead man's spirit was dissatisfied with the verdict. Strange noises were heard emanating from the well and rumours that the man had been murdered and his body dumped in the well began to spread. Nothing was ever proved and no suspects were named, but the noises continue. Some people have even claimed to have seen the man walking to his death, wearing his slippers and dressing gown.

'The Demon Drummer of Tidworth' – an early poltergeist?

The drum had previously been the property of William Drury, a vagrant who had been arrested on charges of causing a nuisance by harassing people while begging – using his drum. Brought before John Mompesson, Drury claimed to be an invalided soldier who had fallen on hard times, and that the beating of the drum had been his particular regimental duty. To verify the story, Mompesson wrote to the colonel of the regiment in question, but had confiscated the drum pending a response.

William Drury had then fled the area, and it was assumed he had used witchcraft to curse Mompesson and his family as revenge for impounding the drum. Authorities across the country were given Drury's description and asked to arrest him and return him to Tidworth.

Following the onset of the 'demon drumming', Mompesson instructed that the instrument be taken outside and burnt – but the banging noises continued. Instead of the drum, the paranormal percussionist was now improvising on furniture and floorboards. Concerned for their safety, Mompesson moved his children's bedrooms to the attic, but the noise moved to stay centred on them – and still only occurred at night. The eldest, teenage, daughter seemed to be the principal focus – the noise only happened when she was sleeping. Events also now took on a more disturbing nature as objects were thrown around and Mrs Mompesson and the children had their hair pulled by an invisible entity.

Six months into the saga, a court official was sent by Charles II with full royal powers and the necessary finances to investigate the matter. A few days after his arrival, a dark figure with glowing red eyes was seen hovering above the floorboards in the house. John Mompesson declared the figure to be a devil and fired at it with his musket.

Further up the Bourne is the garrison town of Tidworth. It was here, in 1661, that one of the most notorious and best recorded series of early paranormal activity occurred – the perpetrator of the events became known as the 'demon drummer of Tidworth'.

The local magistrate, John Mompesson, lived at Tidworth House. On one occasion while he was in London on business for three days, his wife and servants heard a strange knocking noise coming from outside the house each night, which sounded like two pieces of wood being banged together. By the fourth night, Mompesson had returned home. The noise was heard again and he rushed outside armed with a pair of pistols – but with this the noise stopped and nobody was to be seen.

Two nights later the noise was heard again, but this time it emanated from the roof of the house, as if someone was banging on the tiles. Eight nights later the noise finally entered the house itself – this time it was traced to a large drum stored in a downstairs lumber room. Not just a single beat, but hours of rolls and fills, tattoos and marches rang out as if the drum was being beaten by an invisible demon.

The devil vanished and did not reappear. His work apparently concluded, the official returned to the King with his full report – but the demon drumming noises returned to Tidworth House.

William Drury was brought to justice three months later after being arrested in Yorkshire for stealing a pig. He gave a false name but was recognised and returned to Tidworth under an armed guard. He was tried for witchcraft but, perhaps surprisingly, was found 'Not Guilty', despite the evidence of the activities at Tidworth House. He had, however, already been found 'Guilty' in the case of the stolen pig, and was sentenced to two years' hard labour in the West Indies. Following his embarkation, the demon drummer left Tidworth forever.

Modern theories attribute the demon drumming and its associated activities to a poltergeist, rather than witchcraft. Poltergeists often appear when a teenager, usually a girl, is undergoing turmoil. At the time of the haunting, the Mompessons had just had a new baby, and it could be that this the event may have affected their eldest daughter's emotions. Furthermore, the intermittent noise rising to a peak of activity before fading away in time follows a classic poltergeist pattern.

In 1836 the remains of a Roman villa were discovered to the north of Tidworth. A beautiful mosaic was revealed and was donated to the British Museum. However, the archaeological excavations may have disturbed those who once lived there, as a Roman soldier was subsequently often seen marching near the site.

This is probably the ghost that became known as 'Scottie of Tidworth' to many of the service personnel who have been stationed in and around the town. The nickname was coined during the First World War when soldiers regularly reported sightings of the ghost of a man of more than 6ft in height wearing a kilt, standing on the horizon at dusk, or, on misty, rainy days, on the opposite side of the road to the main barracks. There was no record of a Scottish soldier having died in the area in a manner that might lead his spirit to return, and one theory has it that the ghost is not wearing a kilt, but rather the tunic of a Roman soldier.

Another Roman soldier is said to have disturbed young couples enjoying a few late-evening moments of privacy on the quiet road that drops into the valley to the north of Old Sarum. However, given the tens of thousands of service personnel that have lived and died in and around Salisbury – for many of whom it was their last taste of 'Blighty' – it is perhaps surprising that there are so few military ghosts associated with the area.

There is an RAF airfield close to the village of Upavon, but the local phantom is not associated with this establishment – it is the spirit of a strange creature. First seen in 1992, the spectre is usually seen in the fields around the village, although it once appeared in the vicarage garden.

The beast is described as a grey creature, about the size of a wolfhound but with a distinctly cat-like shape and movements. It has been suggested that it may in fact be a real animal, perhaps an escapee puma or similar big-cat from a zoo, circus or private collection. However, no such animal has been reported missing from the locality, and it seems odd that a large predator would spend so long hovering on the edges of a village instead of making use of the wide expanses of the Plain, which is largely free from day-to-day human interference due to military restrictions on access.

Moving down the Avon Valley, the road leading south into Bulford village is haunted by a ghost who whistles. The spirit has been named the 'Whistling Cavalier' but, although he wears a hat with a wide brim, his other attire is more akin to that of an old country worker – the 'bumpkin' or 'yokel' of comic tradition. It may of course be the case that the ghost's hat and generally cheerful disposition invite an automatic comparison with Frans Hals' famous portrait, *The Laughing Cavalier*.

In 1995 a teenage girl reported having been out late one summer's evening when she heard the sound of somebody whistling very loudly and clearly. The tune being whistled was *Greensleeves* – just the first few bars repeated over and over. The girl caught a glimpse of a man in a hat, but he disappeared, and within seconds the whistling faded away.

Ghost Club member Brigadier C. Brownlow reported on the spectral foretelling of a death at nearby Bulford Camp. A former colleague had once told him how, soon after he joined his first battery, he and two other subalterns had become very good friends. When the three men were finally obliged to go their separate ways, they made a pact that whoever died first would come back when the next was fated, and that then these two would eventually come back for the last of them. The first man died of malaria in India, about a year later, and the other died shortly afterwards in a railway accident.

Many years later Brownlow's friend, by now a colonel, called the brigadier in something of a state of alarm, having been convinced that his two dead friends had been seen in the mess at Bulford. Brownlow and a friend, Douglas Johnson (an expert in psychometry) rushed from London to discuss the circumstances with the old colonel. That evening they were invited to dinner at the mess. Later, after the colonel had left to return to his quarters, Johnson and a mess officer witnessed three subalterns dressed in antique uniform standing at a fireplace – one of whom looked like a younger version of the colonel. A few minutes later an NCO

The monument known as Airman's Corner, haunted by a phantom aircraft. (Alan Clarke)

entered the room with a civilian police officer, who reported the colonel had just been killed in a collision with a lorry.

Further west there is another military ghost – that of a machine. Sir Michael Bruce wrote to the *Evening Standard* in 1953 about a strange experience during the Second World War. Shortly before D-Day in 1944, Sir Michael had attended a course at Larkhill Camp, near Durrington. From there, along with three other men and an RAF warrant officer, he travelled around the locality in a jeep, in order to select suitable sites for gun emplacements.

Heading south on the road from Rollestone Camp, the party had suddenly noticed a very small aircraft dive straight down behind a nearby copse. The men raced to give assistance but found no sign of a crash, and could no longer see anything flying above them. Sir Michael had then heard the warrant officer shout, and looked across to see him standing ashen-faced before a stone monument.

The stone commemorated the first deaths from an aeroplane accident in Britain – those of Capt. E. Loraine and Staff-Sgt R. Wilson, who died in 1912 – the first members of the Royal Army Flying Corps to lose their lives. The monument still stands on a green triangle of land at the junction of the A360, A344 and B3086; the junction has since been known as Airman's Corner.

Captain Loraine was aged thirty-three, with a home address in London, and had just been transferred to the RFC from the Grenadier Guards. Staff-Sgt Wilson was an Andover man, aged twenty-nine, and attached to the Corps from the Royal Engineers.

After the accident the aeroplane was inspected and was found to have been in working order, although now smashed to pieces. The inquest heard that the most likely cause of the tragedy was 'over banking'

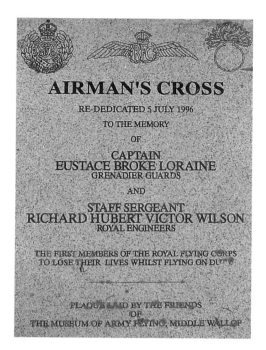

The plaque to Capt. Loraine and Staff-Sgt Wilson who died in the aircraft accident. (Alan Clarke)

whilst attempting a turn, with the result that the machine side-slipped, and then dived at such a steep angle as to be uncontrollable.

By the time officers of the Royal Army Medical Corps arrived on the scene from Larkhill and Rollestone Camps, Staff-Sgt Wilson had a broken neck and was dead. Capt. Loraine was seriously injured, but still semi-conscious, and was removed to the military hospital at Bulford Camp, but died about a quarter-of-an-hour after admission.

As witnessed by Sir Michael Bruce, a small aircraft occasionally appears above the road junction before suddenly nose-diving into the ground. Sightings have continued to the present day, and many futile mobile phone calls have been made to the emergency services as a result.

In 1841 the villages along the Shrewton stretch of the nearby river Till experienced a great flood. Maddington was particularly badly affected and a ghost in a long white dress, who has been seen in several parts of the village, is believed to be that of a girl drowned in the disaster.

On one occasion a man was working in his barn when he looked up and saw a young girl in a long white costume. His daughter, who was also in the barn, saw the same girl at the same time and, without prompting from her father, asked who she was. With this the figure vanished. Revd William Barnard claimed to have seen the ghostly girl inside the church on several occasions, and two village ladies twice saw the same figure glide past the window of their cottage.

Alongside the flooding connection, another theory suggests the girl may have been a novice from an old nunnery that had once existed in the area. However, witnesses have said the girl appears to be wet. Maddington Manor might well have once been connected with a nunnery. Whether the girl came from here or noT cannot be confirmed, but the building does have its own ghost – a crusader who sometimes 'passes through' in the very early morning.

Heading towards Exeter, along the A303 and just before the area known as Willoughby Hedge, there is a junction with the A350. Immediately along this road to the south, on Two Mile Down, high above the village of Hindon, is the home of an apparition that is often witnessed but has never been explained.

This phantom is that of a Victorian-style coach pulled by four grey horses. The coach is enclosed – the passengers are never seen; indeed the coach could be empty. No one has been able to accurately describe the driver, which would suggest he is not particularly gruesome and perhaps still has his head, but there are no local legends to point us towards a reason for the coach continuing to run this lonely stretch of highway.

The ghost of Zeals House, at the edge of the village, which sits just inside the county border with Somerset, does have an explanation – and a tragic one at that. In the eighteenth century, the daughter at the big house fell for a servant from the village. Her father naturally disapproved – the young man was not only unsuitable in terms of class but was, in any case, a somewhat suspicious character that had appeared in the village with no one knowing anything of his background. Despite this, the smitten and headstrong girl continued to see the boy.

One morning the girl was found to have disappeared with a trunk of clothes, her jewellery and a pot of gold. The servant had also disappeared from the village and it was assumed the two of them had eloped. Search parties were sent out but could not find the runaways – the family eventually gave up hope of tracking down the girl and instead prayed that she would return or make contact.

Their prayers were answered, but not in a way the family would have hoped for. Wearing a long, grey cloak, their daughter's ghost began to be seen walking down the stairs of Zeals House, before slipping out of a door, crossing the grounds, skirting around a lake and vanishing into the woods beyond. The ghost was initially seen by servants, who were too afraid to talk, but stories of the spectre eventually reached the family who arranged for the woods to be searched – to no avail.

The ghost was seen by subsequent generations until many years later, in the 1890s, human remains were found in a shallow grave on the edge of a field on the opposite side of the woods near Zeals House – the remains were not accompanied by any jewels or gold. The skeleton was given a proper burial, following which the ghost walked less often, but she is still sometimes

Zeals House, where a ghost has been seen walking down the stairs.

seen around the field where the bones were found and where she was presumably done away with by the conman she loved.

Heading back towards Salisbury along the Nadder Valley, the medieval Place Farm, at the edge of Tisbury, was once owned by the Abbess of Shaftesbury, and is said to be haunted by the ghost of a beautiful nun named Fair Nell. Poor Nell committed the sin of 'looking upon a man' and, as a consequence, her spirit is condemned to walk an area around a tunnel at the farm.

Pythouse, near Tisbury, is haunted by a servant named Molly Peart. Molly had given birth to a child, believed to have been fathered by a member of the household. She killed the child and was executed, but prior to her death, she had placed a curse on the house requiring her remains to be kept there. The body stayed at Pythouse for more than a century before, for some reason, being removed to Preston Manor, near Brighton. With this, odd occurrences took place back at Pythouse: loud, frequent and inexplica-

ble noises and a series of family misfortunes occurred. Molly's skeleton was returned and deposited in the cellars of the house ... and the disturbances stopped.

Old Wardour Castle, south-west of Tisbury, was first built in 1393 for John, Lord Lovel, for use as a stronghold to protect his estates. In subsequent centuries the castle was used as more of a luxury home than a military establishment – so by the time of the English Civil War the building was somewhat out of date as a 'castle'.

Cromwell's army marched into the area in 1643, by which time the staunchly Royalist Arundel family owned and occupied Wardour Castle. At the time, Baron Thomas Arundel was away with the King's Army, and had taken with him those young men from the estates that were fit for action. The baron's wife, sixty-year-old Lady Blanche, was at home with just twenty-five men, a handful of female servants, her daughter-in-law and two small grandsons when the Roundheads approached Wardour with 1,300 men.

Nevertheless, Lady Blanche refused an invitation to surrender – the castle gates were closed, the barrels of ammunition opened and the muskets and swords allocated. The Roundheads used heavy cannons to attack. The 250-year-old stone walls held for a while, but eventually yielded to the heavy iron cannon balls; after several days, a huge breach had been opened. Food and ammunition was running out and, recognising the inevitability of being overrun, Lady Blanche was then persuaded to surrender.

The terms of the surrender were that Lady Blanche, her garrison and servants – and the castle itself – would be honourably treated. However, although the men and servants were released, the castle was sacked and Lady Blanche and her family were taken to a Parliamentarian gaol in Shaftesbury, where she died after hearing that Baron Thomas had been killed in battle at Landsdowne. Lady Blanche

The ghost of Lady Blanche still haunts the grounds of Old Wardour Castle. (Timezone Collection)

and Baron Thomas' son, Henry, became the new baron. Another fervent Royalist, Henry returned to Wardour and attacked the Roundhead garrison now in place to recapture the castle.

Following the defeat of Charles I, Baron Henry fled, penniless, to Europe. The experience and skills he had acquired in the Civil War allowed him to earn a living with armies on the continent, during which time he met and befriended the exiled Charles II. When Charles regained the throne in 1660, Henry Arundel returned to England and the ruins of Wardour; he built a new 'castle' nearby, leaving the ruins of the old family home standing.

The ghost of Lady Blanche soon appeared at Wardour, and walks the grounds into modern times. She is often seen at twilight by the lake at the north of the old castle, walking with small, dignified steps and dressed in a long grey or brown cloak. The new castle was occupied by the Arundel family for several hundred years – later it was used as the private Cranborne Chase School for girls, and has now been converted to luxury apartments. In 1937 the headmistress of Cranborne Chase School, Miss Jukes, witnessed Lady Blanche walking towards the lake. Another spectral presence associated with Wardour is that of a pair of white owls. They are always seen, perching on the roof of the old ancestral home, before the death of an Arundel.

The ghost of a child and a priest are also seen and heard. The Arundels had hidden priests at the castle during times of Catholic persecution, while the younger apparition could be another that originates from the Parliamentarian occupation. It is said that a fourteen-year-old boy asked to join the garrison, but he was in fact a Royalist sympathiser; he was found to be carrying poison to put in the drinking well, and a certain type of paste which, it was believed, when put on guns would cause them to burst when fired. The boy admitted – under extreme duress – to being a saboteur and a spy. His ultimate fate is not recorded, but can perhaps be guessed at.

A Daphne Constantine related a tale of how her aunt, then Miss Dora Gearing, once stayed with another young woman and a party of children at an old rectory in Teffont, in the Nadder Valley. On arrival, the maid had refused to take Dora's cases into her allocated room as she believed it to be haunted. Undaunted, Dora slept in the room for a fortnight without incident, until she awoke in the early hours one morning, dripping with sweat and unable to move her arms and legs – her bed was shaking and the room was filled with the sound of rattling chains.

When she eventually managed to light a candle, the room returned to normal. With that, one of the children burst into the room in a terrible state, claiming he had

'seen something horrible'. On reassuring him and returning him to his room, Dora noticed that candles were lit in the maid's room. Inside the room, the maid was sitting up, crying and moaning about the haunted room. In the morning Miss Gearing mentioned nothing to her adult companion, until it was found that three dogs they had brought with them had all died. The party then returned home.

In his *Notes on The History of Fovant*, a village on the opposite side of the river valley, Dr R. Clay reported on two haunted properties in the village. Oakhanger Barn had been a pair of cottages until 1955, when a brigadier and Mrs Clapp had bought them and converted them into a single property. On a number of occasions the Clapps saw the ghost of an old woman, dressed in grey, walking through the garden from the nearby stream, through the front door, across the hall to the sitting room before disappearing – on one occasion she politely gave way as

Village of Fovant, where two properties are haunted. (Timezone Collection)

Mrs Clapp was trying to enter the sitting room at the same time. Many years earlier Dr Clay had treated a young girl at the cottages, who had described having seen a ghost of similar appearance. In 1932, the village carpenter, Arthur Lever, claimed to have seen a ghost, while he was working on the roof of the cottages, which promptly disappeared when threatened with a hammer.

Dr Clay resided at the Manor House where he had himself seen the ghosts of two family members. One afternoon in the 1920s, his brother Vivian, killed on the Somme, visited the doctor in the dining room of the house and placed a hand on his shoulder, before moving to retrieve something from the mantelpiece, whilst saying, 'I will get it for you mother'. Dr Clay's late mother would herself visit to provide him with guidance in times of concern or indecision after her own death.

At the summit of the steep-sided hills at the western end of the Ebble Valley, high above the village of Berwick St John, sit the remains of an Iron Age hill fort named Winklebury Camp. Local tribes resisted the Anglo, Saxon and Roman hordes here, but there are no ghosts haunting the site from these days – Winklebury's supernatural phenomenon is far more sinister.

It is said that the Devil himself can be summoned to Winklebury Camp by anyone brave enough to climb the hill after dark and run around the earthwork remains of the fortifications seven times. Old Nick will then appear riding a monstrous jet-black horse, and will grant a single wish to whomever has performed the deed. It is not recorded whether anyone has had the courage – if that is the right word – to test this old story. However, the task would be quite difficult as a circuit of the earthworks measure half a mile over broken ground, and running around them seven times in

Winklebury Camp. It is said that the Devil himself can be summoned by anyone brave enough!

the dark would require a great degree of stamina and agility.

The old fort at Winklebury was the target for the Roman legion that features in our next tale. In AD 47, the Roman forces were heading west towards the Severn–Trent line, which they planned to use as the border of their empire. This part of Wiltshire was at the time under the control of a Celtic tribe, the Atrebates.

The Atrebates, ruled by King Tincommius, had initially welcomed the Roman invasion as it overwhelmed their tribal enemies the Catuvellauni, who controlled the lower Thames Valley, but the Romans had pushed on and clearly aimed to subjugate the Atrebates as well.

The celebrated King Caractacus, a member of the Catuvellauni, arrived on the scene. He encouraged the British forces to unite against the invader, using his martial speciality of fast moving hit-and-run raids and ambushes, which left the heavily armoured Roman Legionnaires looking clumsy and bewildered. Caractacus realised that large battles with the legions would almost certainly be lost, but thought that a campaign of resistance would weaken the Roman ability to conquer Britain.

Having gained the trust of the Atrebates, Caractacus decided to set a trap for the Roman XX Valeria Legion as it marched on Winklebury. The location would be at what is now the tiny hamlet of Woodminton, a few miles to the east. Using the steep valley sides for concealment, and then to gain momentum, the combined Celtic warriors launched into the flank of the unsuspecting Roman column.

The battle is replayed in phantom form on bright, moonlit nights. Sometimes only the noise can be heard — the thundering hooves of the horses, the clashing of swords and the cries of the wounded and dying. However, on occasion, the men can also be seen in action — the legion marching in a disciplined manner before the roaring Celts crash into them with their bodies daubed in war paint and their hair coloured with dye and sculpted with mud.

The Celtic resistance to Rome lasted almost ten years before the latter's superior resources finally won out. Caractacus was captured and taken to Rome, where he was paraded through the streets before being presented to the Emperor Claudius. On being asked if he had anything to say before his execution, Caractacus is said to have looked at the opulence all around him and asked, 'If you have all this, why did you want my wooden hut?' Claudius decided to spare Caractacus and he was instead confined to house imprisonment for the rest of his life.

Close to Woodminton, the pretty village of Bowerchalke and its surrounding countryside has inspired two of England's greatest literary knights — Sir William Golding and Sir Terry Pratchett — who both made their homes here, and the village has its own tales concerned with the supernatural.

Applespill Bridge crosses a steam in the village, and is the home of seven phantoms. The ghosts are seen slowly bearing a spectral coffin over the bridge, towards Holy Trinity church. It is natural to suppose that this vision recreates an old funeral procession. However, the legend has it that the ghosts originate from a time when a prehistoric burial barrow, sited high on a chalk hill above the village, was excavated by an antiquarian.

The grave is said to have contained the skeleton of a tall, powerful man, who had been interred with a sword, spear and shield — and a huge cache of gold. The only thing the antiquarian could find that was large and sturdy enough to carry the hoard away was a coffin. He arranged for seven workmen to transport his plunder, and this accounts for the ghostly scene at Applespill Bridge. Believers in karma might hope that the antiquarian met a cursed and painful end, but there is no record of this having been the case.

In the late nineteenth century, an old lady named Mrs Elliott unofficially performed the duties of the Bowerchalke village doctor, nurse and midwife, all rolled into one. Using old country methods and remedies, her services were much in demand. Mrs Elliott never charged a fee, but she was always provided with food by those she helped — vegetables and a cut of meat when the pig was slain.

Soon after Mrs Elliott died, village children began telling of a kindly old lady who would come and sit with them and hold their hands when they were ill. The lady was never seen by adults but nobody who had known her was in any doubt that this was the ghost of old Mrs Elliott. The ghost appeared over a period of fifty years, but has not been seen since the end of the Second World War — perhaps she was content to leave the children's welfare in the hands of the then newly established National Health Service.

A more pitiful ghost haunts the valley slopes to the south of Bowerchalke. Although part of a spectacularly beautiful landscape, these chalk downs can be treacherous when the weather is bad. Many years ago a shepherd was gathering his flock to take them down from the hills into the shelter of the valley, as the weather was turning wintry. A sudden blizzard caught him by surprise and he became disorientated. His spirit still walks the hills where his frozen dead body was later found. Wearing an old rustic's smock, he stumbles around as if lost, plaintively calling, 'I want to go home'.

Meanwhile, a young girl sits at a valley crossroads. The girl is believed to have done away with herself at a time when suicide was still the sin for which one would not be buried in hallowed ground, but at a crossroads. The young spirit sits on her grave, avoiding the gaze of travellers by turning her head away.

St Laurence's churchyard, in the large village of Downton to the south of Salisbury, is said to have a resident ghost that can be raised by running around an ancient tree three times after dark – although there are no modern reports of its having been thus summoned. The large country house in the village named the Moot was originally built in around 1700, but its interior mostly dates from after 1923, when the house was gutted by a disastrous fire. During the fire, a maid named Gwendoline Burnham jumped from an upstairs window in panic and landed on the cook, Mrs Annie Wilson, who was fatally injured. The ghost of the deceased cook is said to haunt the property, although, somewhat confusingly, this spirit manifests itself as a face at the first-floor window.

Another Downton ghost story tells of a man losing control of his horse and cart, and being pulverised by a train as it emerged from the railway tunnel to the north of the village. There is, however, apparently no record of a man having been killed in this way. It may well be the case that concerned twentieth-century mothers invented this tale to keep children away from the tunnel once it had become an exciting, if somewhat hazardous, playground after the closure of the railway line in 1964.

Way up above the village on Wick Down, near the Mizmaze and right at the point of the county border with Hampshire, is Gallows Hill. The hill is believed to be

The ghost of a lost shepherd still walks the hills of Bowerchalke, plaintively calling, 'I want to go home'.

a medieval execution site and possibly also hosted the last moments of Henry Dodington, of Breamore House, located on the other side of the border.

Dodington was hanged in 1629, for the vicious murder of his mother. Having been 'reprehended for some disorderly courses by his mother', Dodington 'drew his sword and ran her twice through, and afterwards, she being dead, gave her many wounds'. It was reported that he would also have 'slain his sister at the same time, had he not been prevented'. He was apparently hanged 'in the sight of the house where he was untimely born' – a description of a location that could well fit Gallows Hill.

Queen Alexandra Road lies well within the modern city boundaries of Salisbury but in 1939, when David Blake's family moved in to a bungalow there named the Dell, it was a semi-rural location. Mrs Tabor had previously lived in the bungalow, throughout the 1930s. The rear of the property faced onto what is now the Bemerton Heath area, but at the time was still open fields. Mrs Tabor's grand-daughter, Jean Harding, had always refused to look out of the rear window of the bungalow as, on more than one occasion, she had seen a man dressed in armour galloping across the fields on a white horse and holding a lance.

When this story was told to a family friend and local historian, Dr Gordon – who had a practice in Castle Street, Salisbury – he explained that the land behind the bungalow had once been a jousting ground and that the nearby Tournament Road was so named in recognition of this.

Richard I ('The Lion Heart') disapproved of the violence involved in the sport of jousting, and in 1194 issued a decree licensing tournaments in only five locations in England. One of these locations was between Salisbury and Wilton, where the Queen Alexandra Road and Bemerton Heath area now lies.

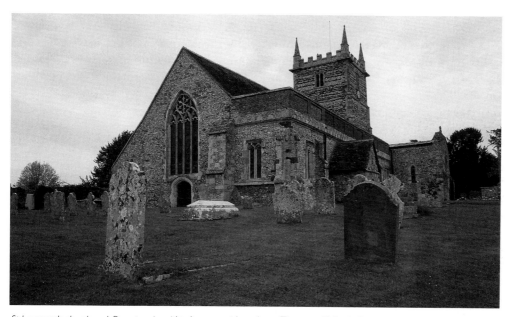

St Laurence's churchyard, Downton, is said to have a resident ghost. (Timezone Collection)

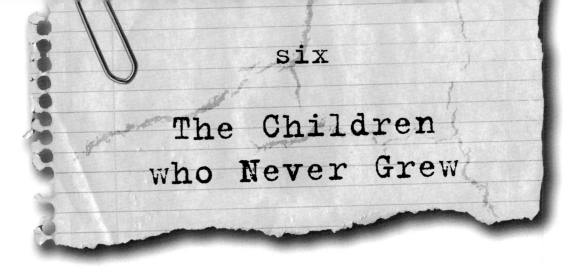

six

The Children
who Never Grew

The Easters and the Haskells

St Ann Street, leading away from Salisbury's Cathedral Close towards the east, is one of the oldest thoroughfares in the city. The street originally provided a route to St Martin's church, which is older than the cathedral itself. Despite this ancient history, the ghosts in this area derive from a much later period.

In August 1842, at the Summer Assizes in Salisbury, thirty-five-year-old Irishwoman Margaret Easter was tried for the wilful murder of her twin children, Mary Ann, who had drowned in a washtub, and Charles, who she was accused of having thrown into a tub, 'wherein was a quantity of hog's wash, whereby he was choked, suffocated, and drowned and there did die'.

Mary Bracher told the court how she was the niece of Ann Bracher, who kept a lodging house opposite the Pelican yard in St Ann Street, but was absent on the day in question, so Mary had the care of the house. Margaret Easter had arrived at the house on Monday 1 August, with her husband and three children; the daughter was seven or eight years old, and the

others were two-year-old twins. On the Wednesday morning the family all ate breakfast together, following which the father went to Salisbury races.

Mary Bracher saw Margaret Easter go in and out of the house several times and, shortly before noon, saw her suckling both the twin children. She then went into her own room to give her children their dinner. About three quarters of an hour later, she noticed that the hogwash tub was running over in the back yard and wondered how this could be, as it had not been near to full.

Mary went to the tub and saw the legs of Charles Easter standing up above the surface of the wash, with his head placed downwards. She ran into the kitchen and said, 'There is a child drowned! Happy, go and take it out for I can't'.

At that time, three other lodgers – Philip Happy, John Hackey and Fanny Harrison – were in the kitchen of the house. Philip Happy ran out, brought the boy in and laid him on the table. John Hackey went upstairs to look for Margaret Easter, calling her several times before she came down. When she finally appeared

St Ann Street, Salisbury, home to the spirits of the murdered children of Margaret Easter? (Wilfred Chaplin)

she cried, 'Oh Lord! My child is drowned! Where is my other child?' Mrs Easter ran straight out to the washtub, then came back inside and said, 'Oh Lord! Here is my other child drowned!'

The door of the house was almost always open and Mary Bracher had looked in the washtub that morning, because a man was due to take it away – and no one had told Margaret Easter that either child had drowned. Mary did, however, note that there was a door close to the tub with a ledge at the bottom, which a child might have been able to use as a step-up.

Philip Happy and John Hackey then brought the other child in. Mary Bracher

told the court that Margaret Easter had been kind and attentive to her children while they were in the house, despite the fact that they were very cross and trouble-some children – except when their mother or father held them in their arms.

Under cross-examination, Mary con-firmed that she had never seen Margaret Easter misconduct herself towards the children. Her eldest child was very ill and on the Tuesday she had taken her daughter to Salisbury Infirmary for advice, and been dispensed medicine. However, although she herself was 'frightened' by what she had seen, she 'never saw the mother cry first or last'.

Philip Happy confirmed that he was lodging at the Bracher's house when the Easter family had arrived on the Monday. On the Wednesday morning he saw Mrs Easter coming into the house with her children. He then lay down and went to sleep in the kitchen. On being awoken by Mrs Bracher, he went out into the yard to the hogwash tub, saw the legs of a child in the tub and took it out. He heard John Hackey call Margaret Easter seven or eight times but it was some time, perhaps seven or eight minutes, before she came down.

He heard Mrs Easter cry, 'Oh my God! Where is my other child?' and reported that she then ran into the yard. She came back into the house and said, 'Oh my God! Both my children are dead!' Happy then went back out into the yard and took the other child out of the washtub. He had noticed that the ledge of the door Mary Bracher had referred to was 7 or 8in from the tub.

John Hackey told the court he had returned to the house at 11 a.m. that morning. He went to sleep in the kitchen and later saw Mrs Easter suckling her twins before falling asleep again. He was awoken by Mary Bracher after the dead boy was brought in. He called upstairs several times, saying, 'Mrs Easter, here's one of your children drowned'. He recalled that she came down very quietly and said nothing, even though he kept telling her the child was drowned. When she got into the kitchen she said, 'Oh my God! Where is the other child?', and she then ran straight to the washtub, although no one had mentioned anything about it.

Elizabeth Jacobs, another lodger at the house, had given the eldest Easter girl some medicine that morning. The other children had cried and Margaret Easter had said, 'Oh! What am I to do with my children? Oh my God, I wish my children were stretched before my eyes before night!' Later, when Elizabeth Jacobs had gone out with her husband's dinner, Mrs Easter was in the kitchen and said her children were 'out backwards'. Mrs Jacobs had enquired as to the children's whereabouts as the house was quiet and they were normally always crying.

John Perry, a gardener, said that at 1.05 p.m. he had seen Margaret Easter in the Pelican yard. She looked around the yard and into the privy and then returned to the lodging house. About a quarter of an hour later he heard the alarm being raised at the Bracher house.

Thomas Blake, the Superintendent of police at Salisbury, had been sent for, and Mr John Winzar, surgeon, had examined the bodies of the children. He had found no marks of violence, no appearance of disease, and neither was there any ground to suppose that poison had been administered to them – they had died from drowning. He noted the children were 2ft 8in high, whilst the hog wash tub was 1ft 8in high.

In summing up, Mr Justice Wightman advised the jury that this was a case requiring the most careful, patient, and attentive consideration. As the prisoner was charged with the murder of her own offspring, they must be satisfied, in order to convict her, that she was the person who had put the children to death. There was nothing in the case that could be used to reduce the offence to manslaughter – the prisoner was either innocent of the charge altogether, or she was guilty of murder. The learned judge then went through the whole of the evidence, 'commenting on it in the most feeling manner, and putting forward every point that could be suggested in favour of the prisoner'.

Nevertheless, the jury returned a verdict of 'Guilty'. Mr Gurney, the clerk of Assize, then addressed Mrs Easter:

You were indicted for the murder of your child. On that indictment you pleaded Not Guilty and threw yourself upon your country, which country has found you Guilty. What have you to say why the Court should not give you judgement to die according to the law?

No answer was returned.

The judge, having put on the black cap, addressed the prisoner:

Margaret Easter, after a most deliberate consideration of your case, the Jury have found you Guilty of a foul and most unnatural murder – the murder of your own unoffending offspring. By the law of God and man, you have incurred the fearful penalty of death. I have not the inclination, nor is it my duty, to aggravate, by any observations of mine upon your guilt, the horrors of your present awful situation. For you there is no hope on earth. Cast then your thoughts beyond the grave and endeavour to obtain from Heaven that mercy which is denied to you on earth. Nothing more remains for me to do than to pass upon you the dreadful sentence of the law, which is that you be taken hence to the prison from whence you came, and from thence to a place of execution, and that you be hanged by the neck until you are dead – and may the Lord have mercy on your soul!'

The prisoner was removed from the bar and taken to Devizes.

Margaret Easter's condemnation created a great deal of sympathy, not only because of the harrowing nature of the circumstances, but also from doubts as to the strength of the evidence on which she was convicted. Efforts were made to save her life through pleas to the Home Office, signed by many Wiltshire Magistrates, and eventually a res-

The judge donned his black cap to find Margaret Easter guilty of murder.

pite was received and the death sentence delayed. Further steps were taken and on 9 September, a free pardon was granted. On her discharge from prison, Margaret Easter was given sufficient money to pay for her return to Ireland, but decided to first travel to Kent to work in the hop gardens, where her husband was waiting with their surviving child.

In subsequent decades, ethereal children have been seen and heard playing around the old corners along St Ann Street in Salisbury. Most are content with their hoops, balls, marbles and alleys, but there is one girl whose cries appear to be less joyful, and who seems to have a different accent, compared to those of the other children. She seems to be looking for something or someone – an innocent game of hide-and-seek? Or will her searching be eternally in vain?

The Easter case has some parallels with another case of child murder that took place more than sixty years later, on 31 October 1908 – Hallowe'en. At 10.30 p.m. that Saturday, while sleeping in his bed at No.40 Meadow Road in the Fisherton area of Salisbury, twelve-year-old Edwin Richard 'Teddy' Haskell was fatally stabbed in the throat.

Teddy was a cheerful, popular and active boy who loved sport – particularly keeping goal at football – despite contracting tuberculosis and, as a result, having his right leg amputated at the age of six. Shortly after the murder had taken place, his mother, widowed laundry worker Flora 'Fanny' Haskell, claimed that a strange man had pushed past her on the stairs of the house and dropped a kitchen knife covered in blood.

Mrs Haskell running, screaming, into the street, said the stranger had run into York Road. Policemen on bicycles watched all roads in and out of the city, whilst local men gathered with sticks and lanterns to search the nearby streets. Bloodhounds were also brought in from Elston Hill at Shrewton to assist with the search, and Scotland Yard sent Chief Inspector Walter Dew on the 8.30 a.m. Sunday morning train from Waterloo. Dew had been involved in the hunt for

Jack the Ripper and would later gain a worldwide reputation when he arrested the notorious Dr Hawley Harvey Crippen as he disembarked from the SS *Montrose* in Canada in 1910.

Throughout the Sunday and Monday, the investigation was focused ever tightly around the murder scene. On Tuesday 3 November a police car arrived at No.40 Meadow Road, and Mrs Haskell was arrested for the murder. Suspicion had arisen from her statements having contradicted those of other witnesses and her clothing having been stained with blood. It was hinted that as a widow Flora had found it difficult to cope financially, and the temptation of Teddy's own savings, which he had been accumulating to pay for a replacement artificial leg, had finally proved too much.

Mrs Haskell was represented by Mr W.J. Trethowan from Nodder and Trethowan,

THE CRIPPLED BOY FOUND DEAD WITH HIS THROAT CUT.

SAW A MAN RUSH DOWN THE STAIRS.

Young Teddy Haskell. Salisbury's most infamous Edwardian murder still remains unsolved. (Illustrated Police News)

The funeral procession of Teddy Haskell. (The Daily Graphic)

The gloomy streets around Meadow Road one week after the murder. The large house at the bottom belonged to Thomas Scammel, who it is believed committed suicide. (Timothy W. Frank Walker & Ann Richardson Whittle)

solicitors of Salisbury. She was tried in Devizes on two occasions for the felonious and wilful killing of her son. At the first trial the jury could not agree on a verdict, and at the second Mrs Haskell was found 'Not Guilty' due to insufficient evidence. The case remains unsolved to this day.

The progress of the Haskell case was comprehensively reported in the local and national newspapers. The lone woman in a state of obvious distress having been accused of the killing of her crippled boy tugged at the heart strings of the nation. In an age when newspapers were the only media available, the minutiae of the trials were reported day-to-day with all the breathless immediacy of modern-day tweets.

Teddy Haskell was buried in Salisbury's Devizes Road Cemetery following a service at which Canon Thwaites officiated. Teddy's school friends from Fisherton filed by his grave and each dropped a bunch of flowers onto the coffin. A floral tribute was provided by the directors of Salisbury Football Club, in the form of a football made of small white and purple violets. Flora Haskell never returned to Salisbury. She died in London in 1920, at the age of forty-six, from tuberculosis.

Even now, the area around Meadow Road can be dark and gloomy – particularly on autumn and winter evenings. The streets are not well lit and the area sits beneath Salisbury's gas holder. One can only imagine how much more foreboding the streets were in the days of coal fires and when steam trains passed through the nearby railway stations.

Historian George Fleming describes the area as 'spooky', and many people have felt an odd presence when walking through here at night. No entity has been seen but the theories are that the presence could be that of Teddy Haskell's unknown killer or his panicking mother, or – perhaps most likely – that of the lad himself, returning home after gamely keeping goal in a kick-about against the gasworks wall in Coldharbour Lane.

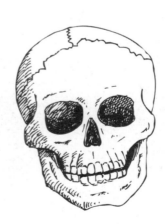

seven

An Uncomfortable Waiting Room

Spirits and Salisbury Station

There were once three railway stations in Salisbury: Salisbury Milford opened in 1847 as a terminus of the London & South Western Railway line running from Bishopstoke (where a connection could be made to Southampton or London); Salisbury Fisherton (GWR) opened in 1856 as a terminus of the Great Western Railway line running from Bristol through Westbury and Warminster; Salisbury Fisherton (LSWR) opened in 1859 as a stop on the Gillingham–Salisbury section

The first Salisbury railway disaster of 1856 resembled a chaotic slaughterhouse.

of the London & South Western Railway Salisbury–Yeovil line. A short branch line was opened in 1859 to serve the city's Market House (now Salisbury Library) and remained open until 1964.

Milford station was closed to passengers in 1859, when a loop was built connecting the LSWR line through to the company's new station at Fisherton, although Milford remained open to goods traffic until 1967. The Fisherton GWR terminus was closed to passengers in 1932 and to goods in 1991, by which time it had long become absorbed into the complex around the modern-day Salisbury station, centred on the original Fisherton LSWR site and buildings.

There is no doubt that railway stations can echo high human emotion – joyful welcomes, tearful goodbyes, the departure for war of young men who would never return. Salisbury has had its share of these echoes, but here the feeling is intensified by the spirits of many who have died in and around the station itself.

On 6 October 1856, just four months after the Salisbury terminus had opened, a loaded GWR livestock train – pulled from Bristol by two engines – passed through Wilton station, to the west of Salisbury. It travelled at a rapid pace which increased to such an extent that when the train reached the terminus, it simply kept going and carried everything in its path along with it.

The four sunken posts against which the buffers of the engine came in contact were snapped off and the floors and joists of the platform, as well as the walls of the ladies' waiting room, which were cut through cleanly, as though, according to the *Salisbury & Winchester Journal*, 'it were the work of carpenters and masons'.

The outer wall of the station was knocked through and the first engine finished up parallel with the walls of the street outside. The rearmost part of this first engine was now resting on the foremost part of the second, which, because of the weight, was embedded in the ground. The impact had caused the tender of the second engine and the first carriage to be tipped up, so that both were in a perpendicular position. The second carriage had also been tipped up, with the third entirely thrown over on to the fourth.

The stoker of the first engine had jumped off on to the platform and struck his head, but was otherwise uninjured. The driver, Mays, had kept to his post and had been carried through to the street unhurt.

The scene within the station resembled a chaotic slaughterhouse as the station was thrown into 'panic stricken ... dismay, confusion, perplexity and darkness'. The gas supply was extinguished in case of fire, so the only light available was from a few candles and dark lanterns – the crowd that had assembled on the platform were stumbling into one another. The foremost engine was now emitting large clouds of steam, filling the station and reducing visibility further.

A fire did indeed break out, caused by the timber of the floors being ignited by the fire from the engine. A hose was immediately attached to the hydrants and water was thrown from buckets to extinguish the flames – without this the station would probably have burnt to the ground.

Nothing had yet been done to remove the animals, and the bodies of the two dead humans had not been discovered. At about 10.30 p.m., sheep began to be removed. A few were alive, but many more were badly mutilated. The majority were crushed to death, whilst some had legs sliced off or broken, and others' entrails were protruding from their torn bodies. Local butchers Messrs Judd and Dowding were called to slaughter the injured animals.

The bodies of the engineer and stoker were found crushed between the tender and the firebox of the second engine, with only the hand of the former being visible from the outside. The Inquiry into the crash concluded that:

> ... the distance between Wylye and Salisbury was travelled over at excessive speed for a train of this description [and] that this speed was continued until the train had arrived so near to Salisbury that the head guard became alarmed, applied his break and kept it on.

Almost fifty years later, in the early hours of Sunday 1 July 1906, the sound of screeching metal and the screams of the injured and dying were again heard emanating from a Salisbury station, as a boat train travelling from Plymouth to Waterloo ploughed into an early-morning goods train stopped on Fisherton Street Bridge at the LSWR station. At the 'curve of death' where the disaster happened, the shrill whistle of a phantom locomotive has been heard at the dead of night, piercing the usually quite area around platform 6. The rail disaster left twenty-eight people dead and many more injured, and the noise of the crash reverberated across the city. Doctors were fetched and people flocked to help the rescue operation. 'As day dawned on Sunday', noted the *Salisbury Times*, 'Salisbury was the scene of an unparalleled catastrophe'.

Forty-three passengers, mostly Americans, had disembarked from the transatlantic liner SS *New York* and had boarded the Ocean Express at Plymouth, crewed by the driver William Robins, fireman Arthur Gadd, a guard, two waiters and a ticket collector. It was common practice for the more affluent transatlantic passengers to take the boat train from Plymouth

(the first point of landfall in Britain) directly to London, thus gaining a day over those who sailed on to Southampton and Portsmouth and made the journey to the capital from there.

The cause of the crash remains something of a mystery, with the inquiry being inconclusive and opinions advanced in subsequent years being no more than theories. As the boat train sped through Salisbury station at around 2 a.m., it was travelling at such high speed that it left the rails immediately after passing through the sharp curve at the eastern end of the platforms, careered along on its side for about 100 yards, wrecked the rear wagons of the London–Yeovil milk train and then smashed into a goods train standing at the station.

Driver Robins and fireman Gadd died instantly, and twenty-four of the boat train passengers were lost. The guard of the milk train and the fireman aboard the goods train were also killed. The station's refreshment room was used as a first-aid station, whilst the ladies' waiting room on platform 4 was used as a temporary morgue – it was here that the firm of Kenyon's (who were just branching out into disaster management) were employed to carry out a mass embalming of the victims.

Mr Dacombe, the head of the firm of John Beeston & Co. in Southampton, was contacted to embalm the majority of the victims. In order to manage the large number of victims involved, he sought the assistance of Herbert and Harold Kenyon for assistance. Together with their staff member Harry Woolcott, and funeral director/embalmer James Goulborn, they travelled to Salisbury.

After the coroner and chief constables had concluded their initial investigation into the accident, the embalming commenced at 1 p.m. on Monday 2 July,

Victims of the 1906 disaster leave Salisbury station for their final destination. (The Daily Graphic)

and continued until 5 p.m. the following day; in total, seventeen bodies were embalmed. Many of the victims had been severely mutilated and the situation was not improved by the extremely hot weather. The embalming was achieved through arterial injection and hypodermic treatment.

On Wednesday 17 July, Herbert Kenyon accompanied five of the bodies on the Cunard steam ship *Carmania* from Liverpool, arriving in New York on 24 July. On arrival, the bodies were examined and reported to be in a good state of preservation.

The ladies' waiting room at Salisbury station is still haunted by the spirits that perished that night, and stories have been told of people sensing a noticeable change of temperature within certain areas of the room. These 'cold spots' are sometimes just a fleeting feeling of freezing cold, but have been known to be more persistent over a longer period.

George Fleming has lectured on the Salisbury rail disaster and has been contacted by people who have experienced the haunting of the waiting room:

It was said that there was always an unnatural chill in that room. I had a conversation recently with a lady whose little daughter, whenever passing through the station, will not use the toilet in that ladies' waiting room. She's never been able to say why, but she just doesn't like going into that toilet. She has to use the toilet on the other platform. It was generally mooted around Salisbury that the waiting room was haunted and cold, but it was rather odd to get confirmation of it from that unusual source.

The station area may also be home to the spirits of two suicides, each of whom enjoyed a degree of notoriety at the time of their deaths.

Before the modern Spire View estate was built on the site of the Eastern Goods Yard, an elderly man, in an elegant Edwardian suit, was regularly seen wandering confusedly about the derelict yard. A similar – possibly the same – unidentified old gentleman has also been seen along St Paul's Road, near the underpass linking the area with Middleton Road and York Road.

The interior of the haunted waiting room at Salisbury railway station. (Timezone Collection)

Could these sightings be the ghost of Thomas Scammell, who had been a prominent resident in York Road and whose unexplained death occurred on the railway, right by the goods yard?

On 20 May 1903, Thomas' body was discovered on the line, opposite his house, just to the east of the station. His head had been severed from his body.

As a boy, Scammell had worked as a labourer and later carried on a business as a broker and antique furniture dealer in Salisbury's Fisherton Street. In later years he speculated in land and buildings.

Scammell acquired more land in the locality and in the 1890s planned a road across the river Avon to connect the area with Castle Street to the east. At that time the land in question belonged to the Hayter Charity Trustees, who for a long time were reluctant to sell it. Scammell failed to persuade the City Council to build the road and eventually took the work on himself.

A toll gate and wrought-iron bridge, the latter of which can still be seen at the end of Nelson Road, was opened in 1899. The last toll was paid on 22 July 1931 when the gate and bridge were purchased by the Salisbury Corporation. A part of the surviving road is now named Scammells Road in his honour.

Thomas Scammell was a Wesleyan in his faith and at one time Liberal in his politics, although he later joined the Conservatives. He served as Chairman of the Fisherton Conservative Club and in the years 1879 and 1893 stood for the City Council for the St Thomas and Fisherton Wards. An 'Open' verdict having been recorded on his death, Thomas Scammell's funeral ser-

The plaque to Thomas Scammell who developed the notorious old gaol ground site at Fisherton. Now he is said to haunt the same area. (Timezone Collection)

the murky world of espionage, certainly the surreal world of the opium den …

In the 1920s, Christopher 'Kit' Wood, son of Julius Wood, the village doctor at Broad Chalke, to the south-west of Salisbury, had seemed to have a glittering career ahead of him. Encouraged by some of the greatest artists of the day, including Picasso, Wood was fast becoming a prominent figure in the world of art, with magazines including *Vogue* and *Tatler* acknowledging his talents.

Christopher Wood had travelled to Paris in 1921 and struck up a friendship with Tony Gandarillas. Gandarillas was a wealthy figure, attached to the Chilean Embassy, who supported Wood financially – but also introduced him to opium, to which Wood later became addicted. Having built a considerable reputation, he returned to spend some time in Broad Chalke during 1928 – three of his best known oil paintings from this period are of local subjects: *Cottage at Broad Chalke, Anemones in a Window, Broad Chalke* and *The Red Cottage, Broad Chalke.*

vice took place in the chapel at the Devizes Road cemetery in Salisbury on 21 May 1903. The chief mourners were his four sons, his brother Andrew, his brother-in-law Mr Simmonds and a Mr Robert Young.

As we have seen in Chapter 3, in the late 1870s, in partnership with Thomas Leach, he purchased the old gaol grounds at Fisherton – the site of so much death and human misery. Did some of this miasma of evil attach itself to the soul of Thomas Scammell?

Perhaps the most famous ghost at Salisbury sation is that of the artist Christopher Wood. This sad phantom has been seen in the vicinity of the Pumpkin Café where the morose figure of this tormented artist haunts the platform.

The story of Christopher Wood introduces us to a mystery which has never been solved, but which has in it a strong whiff of the criminal underworld, perhaps even

The artist Christopher Wood, Salisbury railway station's most famous ghost.

By 1928 Wood had also become good friends with the artist Ben Nicholson, the leader of the Seven & Five group – hailed by the critic Frank Rutter in *The Times* as, 'the most important group of young artists with advanced ideas'. During his return to England, Wood spent some time with Nicholson at his parents' home, the White House at Sutton Veny, near Warminster.

Kit Wood then returned to France, where he painted furiously, achieved a degree of success and became accepted as a member of the second phase of the Modernist movement. He spent the next two years at the village of Treboul in Brittany. His precarious health was further affected by his continued use of opium and by a failed romance. He had fallen for Meraud Guinness, who had joined him in France, but her family had opposed his proposal of marriage. In 1928 Meraud had married Alvaro 'Chile' Gueverra; losing her seems to have weakened Wood further.

In 1930, at the age of only twenty-nine, Wood visited England again. On 21 August, the artist met his mother and sister for lunch at the County Hotel (now the King's Head) in Bridge Street, Salisbury, and showed them some of his latest paintings. A short time later, after saying their goodbyes at Salisbury station, the artist purchased a ticket for Waterloo and a book from a stall on platform 2, and sat down to read. However, he seemed unable to concentrate and began to pace up and down the platform, and then, according to a witness, 'he sort of ran and jumped and dived and screamed' and threw himself under the 2.10 p.m. London-bound train.
He was killed instantly.

Wood's great friend Ben Nicholson was unable to come to terms with the idea that his colleague had committed suicide; he hired a private detective to help explain the tragic occurrence and a strange story emerged.

Two days before his death, Wood had left Gare du Nord in Paris on a boat train

After purchasing a book on this platform, the tragic artist threw himself under the 2.10 p.m. London-bound train. (The Irwell Press Ltd)

bound for Le Havre. He had planned to take the night crossing to Southampton and then a train to London, where he would meet a friend to discuss an exhibition of his latest work. However, a man seemed to recognise Wood on the cross-channel journey, and threatened him. On reaching Southampton Docks, Wood telephoned his mother and sister and arranged to meet them for lunch in Salisbury the following day – he then caught a ferry to Yarmouth on the Isle of Wight and booked into the Pier Hotel.

The detective's report commissioned by Nicholson refers to Wood as 'W' and states that he:

> ... arrived at the Pier Hotel, Yarmouth, Isle of Wight about eleven o'clock on 20 August and was allotted room number nine. He stated he was going to stay for two days. He had with him two suitcases (one of them blue) and three large packets or holders containing, it was understood, pictures. He went to his room with the porter, came down within five minutes and had two whiskies and soda and a sandwich. He then went out. At about 12.40 a.m. he came in again and had a whisky and soda at the bar.

The report mentions how 'W' continued to order alcohol at all times of the day and night, met men in cars that were unrecognised by anyone in the locality, stayed out all night and kept a six-chamber revolver in his overcoat pocket.

Wood left the island on the morning ferry to Lymington and from there took a train to Salisbury – by the middle of that afternoon, 'W' was dead. Although local newspapers reported witnesses as saying that Wood's manner had been strange, nothing was said that shed any particular light on his subsequent suicide. So, it is perhaps unfortunate that Nicholson, on reading the detective's report, decided not to proceed with his own investigations.

The jury at the inquest into Wood's death returned a verdict of 'Suicide while of Unsound Mind', and the coroner remarked that in such instances one searches for a motive but that here there appeared to be none – 'the man was clearly out of his senses'. Christopher Wood undoubtedly believed he was being followed, but this paranoia and his consequent strange behaviour might suggest he was suffering from the effects of his opium addiction. Was this the reason he committed suicide or was something more sinister afoot?

Reddish House, the Broad Chalke home of the Wood family, was later purchased by Cecil Beaton, and later still by rock guitarist Robert Fripp, who lived there with his wife Toyah Wilcox. Kit Wood was buried at All Saints' church, Broad Chalke, a few yards south of the porch, under a flat slab with lettering by Eric Gill. But his soul, haunted in life and haunting in death, still panics its way around the platform at Salisbury station, its last stop in the mortal phase of its existence.

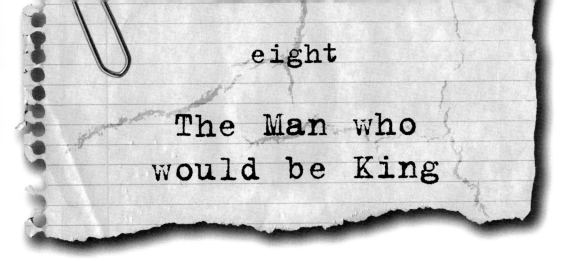

eight

The Man who would be King

Fisherton House Asylum

Fisherton House Asylum, which opened in 1813 and later became known as the Old Manor Hospital, has long been the subject of ghost stories. The tower of Avon House, within the grounds of the asylum in Salisbury's Wilton Road, has long been said to be haunted, and there have been strange stories concerning old wards and underground tunnels. Nursing staff and many other people associated with the establishment have experienced unnatural smells and strange noises – hardly surprising given the history of the institution.

By 1873 William McKave had been confined within the walls of Fisherton House for more than twenty years, prior to which he had been incarcerated at Bedford Asylum for more than seven years. McKave was said to be haunted by a woman named Mary Taylor, with whom he had once cohabited – he was under the delusion that she was still visiting him at the asylum. These delusions were the only reason McKave was being detained; he was not considered to be a dangerous patient.

Interestingly, at the same time as McKave was being haunted by Mary Taylor, other patients reported seeing a woman, dressed in a long black cloak, walking across the grounds where she vanished into thin air – was this the ghost of Mary Taylor?

Notwithstanding this, the *Salisbury Journal* reported that McKave, 'it appeared, was a troublesome patient', their reasoning being that, 'he had repeatedly applied for liberty, and had stated that it was his intention to do something of a nature that would, as he was tired of Salisbury, ensure his being sent to some other place of confinement'.

William Corbin Finch, the proprietor of Fisherton House, said:

> I have heard him repeatedly ask the commissioners for his liberty, and heard him express a wish to be removed to Broadmoor, the Government Asylum for criminal patients. He was not considered to be a dangerous lunatic, although he was in the habit of threatening.

McKave had made numerous appeals to Finch and, more importantly, to the Inspectors of the Lunacy Commission. The Commission, created in 1845 by the Lunatics Act, consisted of six professional inspectors

Fisherton House, Salisbury – home to a royal ghost? (Timezone Collection)

(three physicians and three lawyers) whose full-time job was to make unannounced inspections of the 177 county, provincial, and metropolitan asylums and madhouses located throughout England. As well as passing judgements on these establishments – to the extent that they could recommend closure if they felt it appropriate – the inspectors also had the authority to discharge patients who had been inappropriately admitted.

On 21 May 1873 two Inspectors, Dr James Wilkes and Robert Wilfred Skeffington Lutwidge (the favourite uncle of the author Lewis Carroll), were sent by the commis-

sion to inspect Fisherton House. McKave's frustration and anger at constantly having his appeals rejected had by now reached boiling point. When the Inspectors arrived at Ward 17, where McKave was incarcerated, he pretended to be asleep until such time as they moved to leave, when he leapt forward and struck Lutwidge in the temple. McKave had been concealing a nail in his right hand, the point of which penetrated Lutwidge's skull, such was the force used.

Lutwidge was helped to the house of William Corbin Finch, where he was attended by a Salisbury doctor,

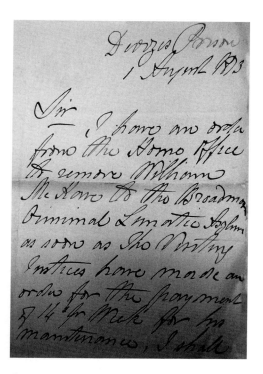

William Martin Coates. He was then transferred to the White Hart Hotel in St John Street. Lewis Carroll, upon being telegraphed, rushed to Salisbury accompanied by the eminent London surgeon, Sir James Paget of St Bartholomew's Hospital. Lutwidge rallied a little and Carroll returned to London but, unfortunately, Lutwidge's condition rapidly deteriorated and he died on 28 May. Lewis Carroll recorded in his diary his 'Dear Uncle's death'.

In court McKave pleaded 'Not Guilty' to murder, but said he did not wish to deny that he had dealt the ultimately fatal blow. After hearing all the evidence, the judge addressed the jury:

> I do not know what inference you may draw from the evidence, but surely you are not to condemn a man to death for an act committed in a lunatic asylum –

seeing that he had been an inmate of it for twenty-one years, and an inmate also of another lunatic asylum for six or seven years previously, and seeing that he has suffered during all that time under chronic mania, and that a gentleman who appears as a witness for the prosecution, and who has been familiar with the prisoner's conduct, his habits, and with the sad disease under which he labours, tells you his opinion is that the prisoner is not responsible for his actions? I think, whatever further evidence may be forthcoming, it will be for you to consider whether you could pronounce a verdict which would consign him to the gallows after the evidence which has been laid before you. If, on the evidence, you think he is not responsible for his actions, and that he was in an unsound state of mind on the 21st of May, it will be your duty to return a verdict of not guilty, in which case he will be kept in confinement during Her Majesty's pleasure. If you desire, however, that the case should go further, do not let anything that has fallen from me prevent you from hearing additional evidence.

After a brief deliberation, the jury returned a verdict of 'Not Guilty' on the grounds of insanity.

Lewis Carroll and his uncle Robert Lutwidge were extremely close friends – despite a thirty-year age difference. They shared many interests, including insanity, and Carroll had accompanied his uncle on visits to asylums. Many scholars have commented on the prominent theme of madness in *Alice's Adventures in Wonderland* and *Through the Looking-Glass*, both written in the decade before Lutwidge's death. Carroll was also fascinated by ghosts and in 1869 had published his longest poem, 'Phantasmagoria':

And as to being in a fright,
Allow me to remark
That Ghosts have just as good a right
In every way, to fear the light,
As Men to fear the dark.

Prince Albert Victor Christian Edward, Fisherton House's most intriguing 'ghost'. (Timezone Collection)

Little more than a year after the death of his uncle, in July 1874, Lewis Carroll began writing what many consider to be his most famous poem, 'The Hunting of the Snark'. Ever since the poem's first publication, it has intrigued and baffled scholars. Many believe it is an expression of his grief at the loss of his uncle, closest friend and intellectual companion – a poem about the Lunacy Commission and the death of Lutwidge following his visit to Fisherton House Asylum.

Perhaps Fisherton House's most intriguing 'ghost' was actually the living body of a man who had only died 'officially' and this legend is that which claims the asylum was home to the Duke of Clarence – Prince Albert Victor Christian Edward (known as 'Eddy').

The duke has infamously been identified as a possible suspect in the Jack the Ripper case. The eldest son of Edward, Prince of Wales (later Edward VII), it is said that Eddy had dark, sexual secrets and, like his womanising, playboy father, it was rumoured that his involvement in many scandalous incidents was hushed up by Buckingham Palace.

The prince was said to have a mild mental disability and to be a rather dull adult, whose intelligence was lower than would be expected of a future monarch. He was also partially deaf and his unusually long arms and neck, which he covered up with high starched collars, led others to call him by the nickname of 'collar and cuffs'.

The official line is that Prince Eddy, then second in line to the throne, died suddenly in the influenza epidemic of 1891–92. However, rumours have long abounded that he was incarcerated in the Fisherton Asylum after being certified insane by the Royal physician, Sir William Gull.

As a boy in the 1940s, Roy Nash lived in Wilton Road in Salisbury, and recalls a favoured pastime of visiting the railway engine yards in Ashfield Road, where inquisitive children could sneak a look over a boundary wall at the unfortunate inmates of the institution as they walked around the lawns. These young imaginations were no doubt fired even further by the stories handed down to the children. Roy's mother and uncle, Jane and Charlie Street, told him of an inmate from their own childhood days – around the dawn of the Edwardian era – who would claim, 'I'm Jack the Ripper, the bugger! I'm Jack the Ripper!'

The last words of Eddy's younger brother, who became George V, are famously attributed as having been 'Bugger Bognor'. Had this particular vulgarity been a guilty favourite amongst Queen Victoria's grandchildren?

Some Fisherton House patients were allowed afternoon passes, which allowed them to visit the centre of Salisbury under limited supervision. Occasionally the patients would break away and staff had to be sent to fetch them back to Fisherton. On one such occasion, a patient was located after entering into the bidding during the auctioning of a house in the city, at which he claimed to be the rightful King of England.

No doubt many asylums had inmates who claimed to be the real Ripper or ruler, but could the Fisherton claimant(s) have been the same man? In 1988, a pipe in the basement cellar of Finch House, a building at the Old Manor Hospital, was shown to a member of staff – the pipe was said to have been scratched with the inscription, 'I am Jack 1888'. One long-standing medical officer of the hospital reported hearing rumours of the Duke of Clarence being incarcerated in Fisherton House, particularly – during the 1970s – from an elderly patient who had originated from Gun Lane in London's East End. The ghost of Prince Eddy has been seen staring from the windows of Avon House, one of the buildings at Fisherton where he was said to have been incarcerated, and strange moans and groans have been heard emanating from the tower of the building.

Avon House with its haunted tower. (Tony Howe and Gina Percy)

In 1970 Dr Thomas Stowell published an article in the *Criminologist* magazine entitled 'Jack the Ripper – A Solution'. The article caused a sensation by suggesting that Prince Eddy was in fact the Ripper. Although referring to the alleged culprit as 'S', Stowell planted enough evidence in the readers mind to leave little doubt that the prince was his man.

According to Stowell's account, Eddy was suffering from syphilis, which he had contracted whilst on tour in the West Indies. This disease eventually drove the prince insane and led him to launch the Autumn of Terror in Whitechapel in 1888. Although the royal family knew that Eddy was the Ripper from at least the second murder, they did not act until after the fourth, when Sir William Gull informed Prince Edward that his son was dying of the syphilitic infection.

The story went that Eddy was then locked away in a private mental asylum but managed to escape and murder a fifth victim, Mary Jane Kelly. He was then re-captured and later died of 'softening of the brain', in a private mental hospital said to have been at Sandringham. However, it is believed by many that the final home of Prince Eddy was, in fact, Fisherton House. It has also been suggested that Fisherton

One of the underground tunnels at Fisherton House Asylum. (Timezone Collection)

was selected because the owners had, for many years, fostered close connections with the royal family. Also, the hospital had an excellent reputation for treating private gentlemen patients and was a convenient distance from London.

Thomas Stowell apparently had access to the private papers of Sir William Gull and used these to formulate his theory. Dr Stowell claimed his main source was Gull's daughter, Caroline, the wife of Theodore Dyke Acland. Stowell had studied under Acland, and had referred to him as being 'one-time my beloved chief' – he was also an executor of Acland's will.

Shortly after publishing his theory in 1970, Thomas Stowell died. His son, another Thomas, claimed that he had destroyed all his father's files on his Jack the Ripper investigations. This, of course, made many elements of the story impossible to substantiate – but it is interesting that both Thomas Stowell and his son resided in Southampton, a relatively short distance from Salisbury and Fisherton House.

Dr Thomas Stowell who named Prince Eddy as the Ripper.
(British Medical Journal)

A royal lunatic, imprisoned *incognito* for life, to conceal his terrible crimes? The monarchy itself threatened if the full, dreadful story ever got out? It all sounds very far-fetched – something Alexandre Dumas might have written about seventeenth-century France!

But here, in England, and in Salisbury of all places? Well, it might be far-fetched, but now consider this: in 1987, many years after the events surrounding this 'ghost' story, it was revealed that Nerissa and Katherine Bowes-Lyon had been admitted to Earlswood Hospital for the mentally disabled in 1941. The two women were the daughters of John Herbert Bowes-Lyon, the brother of Elizabeth Bowes-Lyon – they were therefore the first cousins of our present queen, Elizabeth II.

In 1963 *Burke's Peerage* recorded the sisters as having died in 1940 and 1961. However, Nerissa lived until 1986 and, when Earlswood was closed down in 1997, her sister Katherine was moved into a home in the community. Suggestions of a royal cover-up about the two sisters have been rife ever since, perhaps refined from the experiences of an earlier royal incarceration.

In 1872 Dr William Corbin Finch had entertained Prince Eddy's father – Edward, Prince of Wales – at his home at Bemerton Lodge, near the asylum. By the time Edward visited Salisbury again in 1908, he was King of Great Britain and her dominions, and Emperor of India. His son, the new Prince of Wales, would become King and Emperor as George V in 1910 – but could it be the case that Edward's thoughts turned to his genuine heir as his coach was passing through the crowded city streets – close to the gates of Fisherton House Asylum? And was it the tormented soul of Prince Eddy, in life and then after death, that so many people claimed to have seen then and ever since?

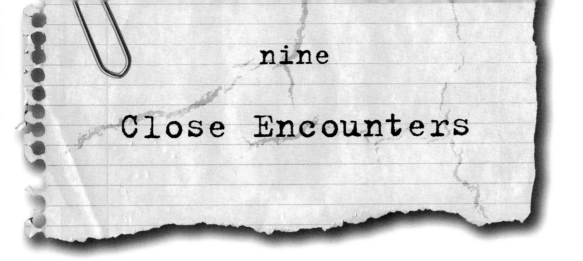

nine

Close Encounters

The Ghosts of Salisbury's Cathedral Close

There is an old Salisbury legend that claims anyone born within the old city walls will return to die there. This curse was said to have been placed by a church official during the Great Plague, when The Close gates were shut on the people of Salisbury, thus denying them access to the cathedral. This measure to avoid the spread of the plague was complemented by the closure of the city's taverns – it is not clear which of these restrictions added most to the citizens' misery.

We have already read how the silken cord used to hang Lord Stourton was once housed in the cathedral, and reappears from time to time. If any of the clergy had harboured Promethean tendencies back in the Middle Ages then other relics housed in the cathedral at that time might have given them a good start.

Alongside the ubiquitous part of the Saviour's cross, the building also apparently held an arm of St Thomas à Becket; some of the hair of St Peter; a tooth of St Macarius; the jaw bone of St Stephen; a finger of St Agnes; and toes belonging to

Ghostly white birds signify the death of a bishop. (Perry Harris)

St Anne and St Mary Magdalene. If the result had evolved into something akin in temperament to Dr Frankenstein's creation, it might have been restrained with a further relic – 'the chain wherewyth St Catharine bound the Devil'.

A further, perhaps less gruesome, relic was found in 1762 when the capstone at the top of the spire was repaired. At the apex a small wooden box had been hidden, containing a round leaden casket containing a piece of woven fabric. The cloth was thought to have been a relic of the Virgin Mary, to whom the cathedral is dedicated – probably deposited there to guard the spire against lightning and strong winds. The spire itself has caused death: in the nineteenth century an unknown sailor was the latest, but not the last, to be successful at the sport of climbing to the top – but just at that point the cathedral bell rang and shocked the sailor, causing him to lose his footing and he fell to his death.

Huge white birds, bigger than swans, have been seen flying around the spire when the death of the bishop or another senior cleric is imminent. The most famous sighting happened in 1885 when a Miss Annie Moberley was walking across The Close and saw the gigantic birds soaring above her. Ignorant of the tradition of 'The Bishop's Birds', she pointed them out to a workman, who filled her in on the legend. This disturbed Miss Moberley, as she was the daughter of the then bishop George Moberley, who had been grievously ill; her father died later that day.

Bishop Moberley's successor, Bishop John Wordsworth, died on 16 August 1911. He had been a popular bishop – a boy's grammar school being a part of his contribution to city life – and his death came as a shock to the citizens of Salisbury. He had been in poor health earlier in the year but things had improved when he rested from his Diocesan duties. On the day of his death, Edith Olivier accompanied the Wilton choirboys on their annual picnic. On their return journey she saw, 'two enormous birds with very long wings ... so brilliantly white that even their shadowed underside shone like water reflecting light'.

Following the death of her father, Annie Moberley later found reference to similar phenomena in fifteenth-century documents, and it seems that white birds must surely have been seen on 29 June 1450. During a peasant revolt known as Jack Cade's Rebellion, the Bishop of Salisbury, William Ayscough, had fled the city when the residents claimed he was spending too much time at Court, as the confessor and secretary of Henry VI, and neglecting his own diocese. The bishop took refuge at the priory church at Edington, near Devizes. He was followed by a mob from Salisbury and dragged, from the altar, up a nearby hill, where they found a heap of Wiltshire flints and stoned him to death. The ringleaders were later hanged and a part of Jack Cade's body was displayed in Salisbury Market Place as a warning to other would-be rebels.

In later times, the bishop would not have to rely on civic justice. James I was a regular visitor to Salisbury, where he would stay in The Close, in a building now named the King's House (in modern times the home of the Salisbury & South Wiltshire Museum). In 1612 James, in parallel with granting the City of Salisbury a Charter of Incorporation, gave a separate and independent charter to The Close. As a result, a number of 'items of correction' were allowed: stocks, a pillory and a whipping-post with irons were set up near the north entrance to the churchyard; a tumbrel was kept in The Close for the conveyance of offenders; a prison, known as 'le grate' was incorporated within the High Street gate to The Close; and a set of gallows

Number 9 in the Cathedral Close is home to a rather unusual ghost. (R. Grundy Heape)

was permanently set up on 'le Busshopes Downe' to the north of the city.

A number of the buildings in The Close are haunted. Close to St Ann's Gate, No. 9 The Close once contained a priest-hole believed to have been the last such hiding-place to be seriously put to use. In later times, during the Corn Law Riots, the mother of a Miss Purvis (then a small child) was brought to the city with two other children, to take refuge at the house, which belonged to the children's uncle.

The children were hidden for several days in a secret room leading off the top attic of the house. In order to reach the room, one would have to touch a section of wall in the attic, which moved to reveal it. At the far side of the room was an escape door leading on to the roof of the building. Although the hiding-place has since disappeared, there is a ghost who was perhaps once concealed here and wishes to repay a favour by keeping the area clean – the spirit makes its presence known by keeping the attic thoroughly dusted.

Rosemary Lane in the shadow of Salisbury Cathedral and another strange event! (Timezone Collection)

The Wardrobe is one of the most haunted buildings in Salisbury. (Timezone Collection)

Opposite No. 9 dwells another friendly ghost in the former home of Dr Turbeville, a celebrated seventeenth-century eye doctor. This ghost helped another previous owner to find legal documents concealed in a wall. Following their discovery, some relevant business was completed to the owner's satisfaction, and the room has had a warm and friendly atmosphere ever since.

Before the First World War, David Blake's mother was in service as a maid in a house in Rosemary Lane, off The Close. The gardener was responsible for filling all the coal buckets each night, in preparation for the next morning, following which he would lock all the doors. On one particular morning, the gardener came downstairs to find the coal buckets not only completely empty, but also spotlessly clean! All the maids had seen the buckets full the previous evening

and no one was able to provide a satisfactory explanation for this strange event.

Backing on to Rosemary Lane is a house fronting on to New Street, close to what is now the Wig & Quill public house. The house was once occupied by Jim and Pearl Shergold, whose baby, whilst sitting in a highchair, would follow someone or something – invisible to others – around the room. At 6.p.m. each evening the Shergolds were disturbed by the doorbell which was of an old-fashioned style, operated by a pull handle and wire which rang the bell on a spring.

The couple eventually tired of this nuisance, which they had put down to naughty children. On a particular day Jim lay in wait by the front door in order to catch the culprit. At dead on 6 p.m., the wire tightened and set off the bell, and Jim raced out – only to be confronted by an empty street. This mystery was never solved. The house belonged to the City Council and, when the Shergolds complained about the bell ringing and other occurrences, they were told that the previous tenants had moved out because of the strange goings-on.

Crossing The Close to the West Walk, a headless Cavalier has been seen crossing the river on a horse, behind the King's House. But perhaps the most haunted building in the entire city is that now known as The Wardrobe, as it was originally used as a store by the Bishop of Salisbury. Dating from 1254, the building is now the home of the regimental museum of the Rifles (Berkshire & Wiltshire). Museum staff and visitors have reported a number of strange events.

Charles II stayed in Salisbury in 1665, to escape the plague, and housed his servants here. The ghost of one of the servants, a lady dressed in grey said to have died from influenza, has been seen sitting and moving around the building. A Cavalier – perhaps he who had crossed the river a little to the south – has also been seen moving around the building; he might technically be a 'poltergeist' as members of the museum staff have reported items having been found moved, or lost, following his visits.

The building was renovated in 1830, and its first occupier was Dr John Grove. The doctor's daughter, Henrietta, married a local Justice of the Peace named James Hussey. The house then remained in the family until James and Henrietta's daughter, Margaret – who was born in the house – died there aged ninety in 1941. Margaret's ghost has been seen in the museum.

Following Margaret's death, the building was used for the remainder of the Second World War as a hostel for the Auxiliary Territorial Service. It was then rented as accommodation by the Diocesan Training College for Schoolmistresses (which was based at the King's House). In 1951 some of the trainee teachers saw the ghost of a lady in green, standing at the foot of their beds and then disappearing through a wall. The next night the women placed their beds together – but still saw the ghost – although she never appeared again.

From 1969 The Wardrobe was unused, until it became a regimental museum in 1981 – the name of which has changed from time to time to reflect army reorganisations. As well as the identifiable ghosts, members of staff have heard a window slamming shut but, upon investigation, have found that in the room in question there was no window – only a bricked-in frame where one had once been. There have also been reports of light anomalies, unexplained ice-cold blasts of air and books jumping from cases for no apparent reason. The attic of the building is also said to often give off strange sensations and an unwelcoming air.

As well as being 'blessed' with a large number of spirits, The Wardrobe seems to have been host to an almost complete range of paranormal activities: the dead servant; the Cavalier – who might also be a poltergeist; the harmless long-term occupier who doesn't want to leave; the mysterious 'lady in grey'; walking through walls; unexplained noises; strange lights; cold air; moving objects.

As we have seen, these types of phenomena are reported regularly over the whole of Salisbury and South Wiltshire. Some can perhaps be explained in 'rational' terms; some are somewhat bolstered by a theory – albeit often unproven; some seem to have no basis in fact or history, but this doesn't make them any less 'real'. We hope you have enjoyed our collection of tales and that they might encourage you to explore your interest further. Please be careful!

Where we Heard our Stories

Individuals

David Blake
Diana Cannons
Kathie Child
George Fleming
Justina Miller
Roy Nash
Dave Taylor

Books

Ash, R., *Discovering Highwaymen: A Gallery of Rogues* (Shire Publications, 1970)

Baker, A., *History Beneath Our Feet: A Guide To The Devizes Road and London Road Cemeteries* (Salisbury District Council, 1993)

Daniels, P., *The Archive Photographs Series: Salisbury* (Chalford Publishing Co., 1995)

Daniels, P., *Salisbury in Old Photographs: A Second Selection* (Alan Sutton, 1988)

Daniels, P., *Salisbury in Old Photographs: A Third Selection* (Alan Sutton, 1992)

Hilliam, D., *A Salisbury Miscellany* (Sutton Publishing, 2005)

Howe, T. and Percy, G., *The Old Manor Salisbury: A Glimpse into the Past* (Salisbury Health Care NHS Trust, 2000)

Jowitt, R.L.P., *British Cities: Salisbury* (Batsford, 1951)

Light, A. & Ponting, G., *Breamore Yesterday and Today* (Charlewood Press, 2005)

Matthews, R., *Haunted Places of Wiltshire* (Countryside Books, 2004)

Moody, J.B. and Purvis, B.S., *If I Did It … I Don't Remember: Salisbury's Edwardian Murder Mystery* (Hob Nob Press, 2008)

Oakley, M., *Wiltshire Railway Stations* (The Dovecote Press, 2004)

Shortt, H. (ed.) *City of Salisbury* (SR Publications, 1957)

Spring, R., *Salisbury Cathedral* (Unwin Hyman, 1987)

Street, P., *Portrait of Wiltshire* (Robert Hale Ltd, 1971)

Underwood, P., *Ghosts of Wiltshire* (Bossiney Books, 1989)

Watts, K., *Figures in a Wiltshire Scene* (Hob Nob Press, 2002)

Whitlock, R., *Wiltshire* (Batsford, 1976)

Churches of South East Wiltshire (Royal Commission on the Historical Monuments of England, 1987)

Salisbury in Detail (Salisbury Civic Society, 2009)

From The Sarum Chronicle

(Hobnob Press)

Shillingford, E., 'The Greencroft', issue 6, 2006

Richards, D., 'Anne Bodenham: Her Trial for Witchcraft in Salisbury, 1653', issue 9, 2009

Wright, T., 'A Peculiar Kind of Lodging House: Life and Death in Fisherton Gaol, 1800-1850', issue 10, 2010

Howells, J., 'John Wordsworth 1843-1911', issue 11, 2011

Newspapers

Evening Standard
Salisbury & Winchester Journal
Salisbury Times

Others

Wikipedia

Kenyon's Newsletter

The Rai d'Or: A Short History of a Historic Tavern

Dowding, W., *Fisherton Gaol: Statistics of Crime* (1855)

Discussions of Great Import in the public houses of Salisbury

The staff of The Wardrobe Museum, Salisbury

Local Studies Library, Salisbury

Special Thanks

We would like to thank Perry Harris for providing the illustrations for this publication.

More details can be found at:
Twitter @uhperry
www.perryharris.com

About the Authors

JEREMY 'Frogg' Moody was born in Salisbury where he still resides. In 2004 he formed The Salisbury Timezone Group to research and record social life and historical events from the city's past through books, theatre, music, lectures and exhibitions.

Frogg has co-authored *If I Did It ... I Don't Remember* (Hob Nob Press, 2008)and *Jack the Ripper: The Suspects* (The History Press, 2011), edited *Written and Red* (Timezone, 2009), and been involved – as editor – in a Salisbury music magazine, *Beat Route*. In June 2010 Frogg was presented with the British Association for Local History Award for his contribution to the study of local history.

Frogg is also a talented musician and composer, and a well-known face on the local music scene himself, having played with several local bands. He is the musical composer of the internationally acclaimed stage musicals 'Yours Truly', 'Jack The Ripper' and 'Daughter of Destiny – The True Titanic Love Story'. www.timezonepublishing.com

RICHARD Nash has spent most of his life in Downton, near Salisbury. During the eighties and early nineties he produced *The Rambler*, which might loosely be described as a 'lifestyle' fanzine, and which remains something of a cult in the area. He has contributed articles, reviews and football match reports to *Shindig!*, *Record Collector*, *Beat Route*, the *Salisbury Journal* and various fanzines, and also operates www.southwilts. com/site/bluemoonraker, a website concerned with the history of the Salisbury music scene. Richard has also co-authored booklets about the Downton Heritage Trail (2009) and Downton Cuckoo Fair (2011), and operates a website about the buildings of Downton (www.southwilts.com/site/downtonbuildings).

Frogg and Richard's previous joint ventures have been:

'Hold Tight! – Voices of the Sarum Sound 1945-1969' (Timezone 2007)
'Endless Beat – Voices of the New Sarum Sound 1970-1999' (Timezone 2010)
'Walls of Sound' (Major Exhibition at Salisbury & South Wiltshire Museum) (October 2010-January 2011)

They have also given presentations to various groups and are planning a series of new talks and events on various aspects of Salisbury's history in the near future.

Index of
People and Places

If you enjoyed this book, you may also be interested in…

Haunted Winchester
MATTHEW FELDWICK

Drawing on historical and contemporary sources, *Haunted Winchester* contains a chilling range of ghostly accounts. This selection includes tales of spectral monks at Winchester Cathedral and phantom horses in the Cathedral Close, as well as stories of the Eclipse Inn where Dame Alice Lisle, condemned by Judge Jefferies, still walks. This phenomenal gathering of ghostly goings-on is bound to captivate anyone interested in the supernatural history of the area.

978 07524 3846 7

Haunted Southampton
PENNY LEGG

Explore the darkest secrets of Southampton's past with this collection of stories telling of the apparitions that have haunted residents of the city for centuries. From the Roman soldiers who pervade Bitterne Manor to the Grey Lady at the Royal Victoria Country Park, the city is host to countless spirits not yet departed. No matter where you are in the city, incidents of unexplained phenomena have taken place nearby.

978 07524 5519 8

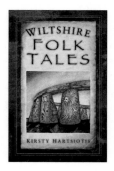

Wiltshire Folk Tales
KIRSTY HARTSIOTIS

These lively folk tales from one of Britain's most ancient counties are vividly retold by local storyteller Kirsty Hartsiotis. Their origins lost in the oral tradition, these stories from Wiltshire reflect the wisdom of the county and its people. Discover Merlin's trickery, King Alfred's bravery, dabchicks and the devil, the flying monk of Malmesbury and the ravenous maggot of Little Langford. These tales bring alive the landscape of the country's ancient barrows, stone circles and rolling hills.

978 07524 5736 9

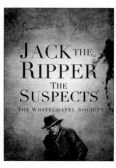

Jack the Ripper: The Suspects
THE WHITECHAPEL SOCIETY

The murders of 1888 remain unsolved and hundreds of theories have been suggested as to the killer's identity. However, many of the suggestions remain ill-informed – until now! Based on indisputable facts and concrete evidence, the cases put forward in this collection allow readers to decide who they believe is the man behind the myth. With each chapter discussing a separate suspect in detail, this book is the ultimate guide to the most famous criminal investigation in British history.

978 07524 6286 8

Visit our website and discover thousands of other History Press books.

www.thehistorypress.co.uk